THE FALL OF
Advertising

ALSO BY AL AND LAURA RIES

The 22 Immutable Laws of Branding

The 11 Immutable Laws of Internet Branding

ALSO BY AL RIES

Focus: The Future of Your Company Depends on It

The 22 Immutable Laws of Marketing*

Horse Sense*

Bottom-Up Marketing*

Marketing Warfare*

Positioning: The Battle for Your Mind*

*WITH JACK TROUT

THE FALL OF
Advertising

and

THE RISE OF
PR

AL RIES _and_
LAURA RIES

HarperBusiness
An Imprint of HarperCollins_Publishers_

HarperCollins books may be purchased for educational, business, or
sales promotional use. For information, please
e-mail the Special Markets Department at
SPsales@harpercollins.com.

First HarperBusiness paperback edition published 2004.

Designed by Jennifer Ann Daddio

Library of Congress has catalogued the hardcover edition as follows:

Ries, Al.
The fall of advertising and the rise of PR /
Al Ries and Laura Ries.
p. cm.
ISBN 0-06-008198-8
1. Advertising. 2. Brand name products.
3. Public Relations. I. Ries, Laura. II. Title.
HF5823 .R642 2002
659—dc21   2002023294

ISBN 0-06-008199-6 (pbk.)

HB 05.03.2021

Dedicated to

CONRAD RIES BROWN,

*our son and grandson, who arrived the day
after we completed the manuscript*

Contents

PART TWO

The Rise of PR

PART THREE

A New Role for Advertising

PART FOUR

The Differences Between Advertising and PR

PART FIVE

Postscripts

Features

THE POSITIONING ERA COMETH

The changes that have come about in advertising strategies as a result of "the positioning era," how it came to be and what it means to us now are examined in this first in a three-part series by two spacey principals, both alumni of General Electric's advertising and sales promotion department. Since their GE days, Mr. Ries was an account supervisor at Needham, Louis & Brorby and Marsteller Inc. before becoming president of Ries Cappiello Colwell, and Mr. Trout was a divisional ad manager for Uniroyal. He now is vp and director of marketing services for Ries Cappiello.

BY JACK TROUT AND AL RIES
Ries Cappiello Colwell

Today it has become obvious that advertising is entering a new era. An era where creativity is no longer the key to success.

The fun and games of the '60s have given way to the harsh realities of the '70s. Today's marketplace is no longer responsive to the kind of advertising that worked in the past. There are just too many products, too many companies, too much marketing "noise."

To succeed in our over-communicated society, a company must create a "position" in the prospect's mind. A position that takes into consideration not only its own strength and weaknesses, but those of its competitors as well.

Advertising is entering an era where strategy is king.

A Tale of Two Ads

If you had to pick an official date to mark the end of the last advertising era and the start of the new one, your choice would have to be Wednesday, April 7, 1971. In the *New York Times* that day was a full-page ad that seemed to generate very little excitement in the advertising community.

But then, an abrupt change in the direction of an industry isn't always accompanied by the blowing of bugles. You sometimes need the vantage point of history to realize what has happened.

The ad that appeared that spring morning in 1971 was written by David Ogilvy. And it's no coincidence that the architect of one era called the time for the next.

In the ad, the articulate Mr. Ogilvy outlined his 38 points for creating "advertising that sells."

In first place on his list was a point Mr. Ogilvy called "the most important decision." Then he went on to say, "The results of your campaign depend less on how we write your advertising than on how your product is positioned."

• Blow the bugles, the positioning era has begun.

Five days later, in the *New York Times* and in ADVERTISING AGE, another ad appeared that confirmed the fact that the advertising industry was indeed changing direction. Placed by Rosenfeld, Sirowitz & Lawson, the ad listed the agency's four guiding principles.

In first place was, you guessed it. According to Ron Rosenfeld, Len Sirowitz and Tom Lawson, "Accurate positioning is the most important step in effective selling."

In the '50s, hard sell ads predominated.

In the '60s, creativity came into vogue.

In the '70s, strategy will be king.

Suddenly the word and the concept was in everybody's ads and on everybody's lips. Hardly an issue of ADVERTISING AGE passes without some reference to "positioning."

You Can't Beat 'em Head-On

In spite of Madison Ave.'s current love affair with positioning, the concept had a more humble beginning.

In 1969, one of us (Jack Trout) wrote an article entitled "Positioning is a game people play in today's me-too marketplace," which appeared in the June, 1969, issue of *Industrial Marketing*. The article made predictions and named names, all based on the "rules" of a game called positioning.

One prediction, in particular, turned out to be strikingly accurate. As far as RCA and computers were concerned, "a company has no hope to make progress head-on against the position that IBM has established."

The operative word, of course, is "head-on." And while it's possible to compete successfully with a market leader (the article suggested several approaches), the rules of positioning say it can't be done "head-on."

Three years ago this raised a few eyebrows. Who were we to say that powerful, multi-billion-dollar companies couldn't find happiness in the computer business if they so desired?

Desire, alas, was not enough. Not only RCA, but also General Electric bit the IBM dust.

With two major computer manufacturers folding one right after another, the urge to say, "I told you so," was irresistible.

Last November, a follow-up article, "Positioning revisited: Why didn't GE and RCA listen?" appeared in the same publication.

We're an Over-Communicated Society

As GE and RCA found out, advertising doesn't work anymore. At least, not like it used to. One reason may be the noise level in the communications jungle.

The per-capita consumption of advertising in the U.S. is approaching $100 a year. And while no one doubts the advertiser's financial ability to dish it out, there's some question about the consumer's mental ability to take it all in.

Each day, thousands of messages compete for a share of the prospect's mind. And, make no mistake about it, the mind of the battleground. Between six inches of grey matter is where the advertising war takes place. And the battle is rough, with no holds barred and no quarter given.

The new ball game can prove unsettling to companies that grew up in an era where any regular advertising was likely to bring success. This is why you see a mature, sophisticated company like Bristol-Myers run through millions of dollars trying to launch me-too products against strongly dug-in competition. (If you haven't noticed, Fact, Vote and Resolve are no longer with us.)

To understand why some companies have trouble playing in today's positioning game, it might be helpful to take a look at recent communications history.

'50s Were the Product Era

Back in the '50s, advertising was in the "product" era. In a lot of ways, these were the good old days when the "better mousetrap" and some money to promote it were all you needed.

It was a time when advertising people focused their attention on product features and customer benefits. They looked for, as Rosser Reeves called it, the "Unique Selling Proposition."

But in the late '50s, technology started to rear its ugly

This is the first in a series of three articles introducing the positioning concept to readers of Advertising Age. It appeared in the April 24, 1972, issue of the magazine.

Introduction

Thirty years ago, Al cowrote a series of articles for *Advertising Age* entitled "The Positioning Era Cometh." They were an instant hit. Almost overnight, *positioning* became a buzzword among advertising and marketing people.

If we were writing the same articles for the same publication today, our title would have to be "The Public Relations Era Cometh." Wherever we look, we see a dramatic shift from advertising-oriented marketing to public-relations-oriented marketing.

You can't launch a new brand with advertising because advertising has no credibility. It's the self-serving voice of a company anxious to make a sale.

You can launch new brands only with publicity or public relations (PR). PR allows you to tell your story indirectly through third-party outlets, primarily the media.

PR has credibility. Advertising does not. PR provides the positive perceptions that an advertising campaign, if properly directed, can exploit.

When we counsel clients, we normally recommend that any new marketing program start with publicity and shift to advertising only after the PR objectives have been achieved. For managers indoctrinated in an advertising culture, this is a revolutionary idea. For others it's a natural evolution in marketing thinking.

A Continuation of PR

Advertising should follow PR in both timing and theme. Advertising is a continuation of public relations by other means and should be started only after a PR program has run its course. Furthermore, the theme of an advertising program should repeat the perceptions created in the mind of the prospect by the PR program.

Nor is the advertising phase of a program something to be taken lightly. An advertising program should be launched only on behalf of a strong brand and only by a company that can afford the commitment an advertising campaign demands.

Advertising people sometimes put down the PR function as a secondary discipline, useful only in a crisis or perhaps to publicize the latest advertising campaign. Nothing could be further from the truth.

For most companies today, PR is far too important to take a backseat to advertising. In many ways the roles are reversed. PR is in the driver's seat and should lead and direct a marketing program. Hence the title of our book: *The Fall of Advertising and the Rise of PR*.

Advertising Is Dead. Long Live PR

But how can advertising be dead if there is so much of it? You see advertisements everywhere you look.

It's like painting. Painting is also dead even though painting is more popular today than it ever was.

When it comes to painting, its "death" is not the death of painting itself, but the death of its function as a representation of reality.

The years that followed Louis-Jacques-Mandé Daguerre's invention of the daguerreotype might have been called "the fall of painting and the rise of photography." In the same sense, advertising has lost its function as a brand-building tool and lives on as art.

This doesn't mean that advertising has no value. The value of art is in the eye of the beholder. It only means that when a functional discipline becomes art, it loses function and therefore its ability to be objectively measured.

The Value of a Candle

How do you measure the value of a candle? You can't measure its value by light output, since the candle has lost its function as a means of lighting a room. The years that followed Thomas Alva Edison's invention of the incandescent lamp might have been called "the fall of the candle and the rise of the lightbulb."

Yet every night all over America millions of candles are burning. No romantic dinner is complete without candles on the table. Individual candles are sold for $20 or $30 each, much more than a lightbulb. Unlike an electric bulb, the value of a candle has no relationship to its light output. Like the fireplace and the sailing ship, the candle has lost its function and turned into art.

Every form of artwork has its passionate defenders. They will strenuously argue over the value of an individual piece of artwork because there isn't an objective way to measure its value.

The Value of an Advertisement

Advertising fits the same pattern. The ad advocates will emotionally defend their work on the basis of enhancing the equity of the brand or building brand value or creating an emotional bond with consumers or inspiring and motivating the sales force.

To a certain extent, all of this is true, but it can't be objectively measured because advertising is art. It has lost its communications function.

Advertising's value is in the eye of the CEO or the COO or the marketing manager. How much value would you assign the million-dollar painting that hangs in the boardroom? The same logic you apply to the painting can also be applied to your company's advertising.

Our opinion: Advertising is not worth what it costs . . . with one exception. And it's a big exception. When advertising serves a functional purpose, then advertising has a real value. But what is that functional purpose?

The purpose of advertising is not to build a brand, but to defend a brand once the brand has been built by other means, primarily public relations or third-party endorsements.

Don't underestimate the importance of this defensive function. Most companies spend way too much money trying to build brands with advertising (when they should be using that money for PR) and way too little money defending their brands with advertising after they have been built.

Creating a brand and defending a brand are the two major functions of a marketing program. PR creates the brand. Advertising defends the brand. Ironically, advertising people have spent so much time and energy on the brand-building process that they are often not emotionally capable of fighting a defensive marketing war.

The Value of Creativity

What about creativity, the buzzword of the advertising community for as long as we can remember? Creativity, according to a common definition, is the search for the new and different. The emphasis is on being original.

But the "new and different" is not how you defend a brand. To defend a brand you need to "reaffirm" the brand's core values. You need to run advertising that "resonates" with consumers. You need consumers to think, "Yes, that's what the brand stands for."

Creativity is the last thing a brand needs once a brand has been established in the mind.

It's PR that needs to be creative. It's PR that needs to be new and different. It's PR that needs to be original. The best way to establish a brand is to create a new category, and creating a new category requires creative thinking of the highest order. This is a revolutionary concept in the sense that it goes against conventional thinking.

The Conventional Approach

Most products and services are marketed following a four-step strategy:

1. The company develops a new product or service.
2. The company researches the new product or service to make sure it offers consumers a significant benefit.
3. The company hires an advertising agency to launch the new product or service with a "big bang" advertising campaign.
4. Over time the advertising builds the new product or service into a powerful brand.

The four steps in the process have achieved icon status in the annals of business history: Development, Research, Advertising, and Branding. In theory, there is nothing wrong with the four-step process, except for its unfortunate acronym, DRAB.

In practice, there is one weak link. The crucial step is getting the brand name (and that's what it stands for) into the mind of the consumer. You can't build a brand if you can't win the battle for the mind.

The weak link is advertising.

Advertising has lost its power to put a new brand name into the mind. Advertising has no credibility with consumers, who are increasingly skeptical of its claims and whenever possible are inclined to reject its messages.

The PR Approach

Obviously some products and services have gotten into the prospect's mind and become big brands. How did they do this?

With publicity.

All the recent marketing successes have been PR successes, not advertising successes. To name a few: Starbucks, The Body Shop, Amazon.com, Yahoo!, eBay, Palm, Google, Linus, PlayStation, Harry Potter, Botox, Red Bull, Microsoft, Intel, and BlackBerry.

A closer look at the history of most major brands shows this to be true. As a matter of fact, an astonishing number of well-known brands have been built with virtually no advertising at all.

Anita Roddick built The Body Shop into a worldwide brand without any advertising. Instead she traveled the world looking for ingredients for her natural cosmetics, a quest that resulted in endless publicity.

Until recently Starbucks didn't spend a hill of beans on advertising either. In its first ten years, the company spent less that $10 million (total) on advertising in the United States, a trivial amount for a brand that delivers annual sales of $1.3 billion today.

Wal-Mart became the world's largest retailer, ringing up sales approaching $200 billion, with little advertising. Sam's Club, a

Wal-Mart sibling, averages $56 million per store with almost no advertising.

In the pharmaceutical field, Viagra, Prozac, and Vioxx became worldwide brands with almost no advertising.

In the toy field, Beanie Babies, Tickle Me Elmo, and Pokémon became highly successful brands with almost no advertising.

In the high-technology field, Oracle, Cisco, and SAP became multibillion-dollar companies (and multibillion-dollar brands) with almost no advertising.

We're beginning to see research that supports the superiority of PR over advertising to launch a brand. A recent study of ninety-one new-product launches shows that highly successful products are more likely to use PR-related activities than less successful ones. Commissioned by Schneider & Associates in collaboration with Boston University's Communications Research Center and Susan Fournier, an associate professor of marketing at the Harvard Business School, the study is believed to be the first of its kind.

"We learned that the role of PR, while underutilized, was extremely significant when leveraged," said the study.

In spite of PR's many successes, there is still the perception inside the corporation that marketing does not include public relations.

Marketing Means Advertising

For many corporate managers, it's true that marketing is synonymous with advertising—not PR. "Mass marketing requires mass communications, which require mass advertising" was the old formula. When someone mentions a marketing program, the first thought is "Where are we going to advertise and how much money do we have in the advertising budget?"

If you walk into a bookstore like Barnes & Noble, you will find the advertising books in a section called "Marketing & Advertising." In fact, the category is loaded with advertising books. After all, the primary function of a marketing department is perceived to be advertising.

Don't expect to find a "Marketing & Public Relations" section at any bookstore. The PR books, if you can find any, are buried in the "Marketing & Advertising" section along with all those advertising books.

The view inside the corporation is similar to the view inside your neighborhood bookstore. The emphasis in most corporations is on advertising, with public relations considered a secondary discipline, if it is considered at all.

Marketing means advertising and everybody knows what advertising means.

Advertising Means Big Bucks

This is particularly true when a company is considering the launch of a new brand. A "go/no go" decision is often based on the advertising cost of launching the brand. When even a modest national advertising campaign for a new consumer product in the United States can run $50 million or so, these decisions are not taken lightly.

"It's a good idea," many clients have told us, "but we can't afford the money needed to launch the brand." Their thinking is skewed by the stories they read in the media.

- Pepsi-Cola spends $100 million to launch Pepsi One.
- Andersen Consulting spends $150 million to launch its new name, Accenture.
- Bell Atlantic spends $140 million to launch its new name, Verizon.

- Bell South Mobility spends $100 million to launch its new name, Cingular.

In this overcommunicated society of ours, the cost of launching a new brand is perceived to be in the same category as orthodontics— an expensive proposition that can hopefully be avoided by launching a line extension instead. That's why America is loaded with line extensions and starved for new brands.

Nine out of ten new supermarket products, for example, are line extensions and not new brands. And the same situation exists in drugstores, department stores, and all types of retail establishments.

Equating the launch of a new brand with advertising is a serious marketing error. Advertising lacks the one ingredient that a new brand needs if it is to get off the ground.

Advertising Lacks Credibility

Why would anyone pay attention to a message about a brand they have never heard of? Where is the believability in such a message?

If someone calls you on the phone and says, "You don't know me, you don't know my products, you don't know my company, but I would like to make an appointment to try to sell you something," you would immediately hang up the phone.

On the other hand, if someone calls you on the phone and says, "You are a customer of Saks Fifth Avenue and Saks is having a cocktail party to introduce a new line of designer clothes," you might be tempted to show up. Saks Fifth Avenue has credibility in your mind. It's a name you know.

Publicity provides the credentials that create credibility in the advertising. Until a new brand has some credentials in your mind, you are going to ignore its advertising.

If you are going to be successful in building a brand, you need to manage both public relations and advertising properly. The general rule is, Never run advertising until the major publicity possibilities have been exploited.

Publicity First, Advertising Second

Advertising doesn't build brands, publicity does. Advertising can only maintain brands that have been created by publicity.

The truth is, advertising cannot start a fire. It can only fan a fire after it has been started. To get something going from nothing, you need the validity that only third-party endorsements can bring. The first stage of any new campaign ought to be public relations.

War and marketing have many similarities. Military generals who fight today's war with the last war's weapons are no different from marketing generals who fight today's marketing war with advertising when they should be using PR.

Yesterday it was armor. Today it's airpower. Yesterday it was advertising. Today it's PR.

With publicity assuming the major role in most new-product launches, whom do clients consult with on strategic questions? More and more, they hesitate to ask their advertising agencies for advice because they know the advice they are going to receive. So they go it alone without outside help. Or they invite consultants like us to work with them on strategic marketing issues including PR.

In the future, clients will be looking to public relations firms to help them set the strategic directions for brands, and advertising will be forced to follow the lead of PR.

In the future, you can expect explosive growth in the PR industry. You can also expect to find a new respect for public relations both inside and outside the corporation.

In the future, you can expect to hear howls of anguish from the advertising industry. And it's not just the money. Even more important to advertising agency executives is the potential loss of their traditional role as marketing partners.

Marketing has entered the era of public relations.

PART ONE

The Fall of Advertising

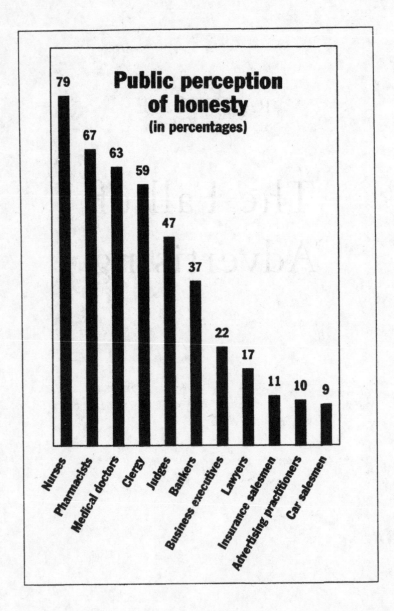

Public perception of honesty
(in percentages)

Nurses	79
Pharmacists	67
Medical doctors	63
Clergy	59
Judges	47
Bankers	37
Business executives	22
Lawyers	17
Insurance salesmen	11
Advertising practitioners	10
Car salesmen	9

Advertising *and* Car Salesmen

Not long ago, four New York City nurses were killed when they drove off the top of a motel's five-story parking garage. The story made all of the New York papers, including the front page of the *New York Post*. Sixteen hundred mourners attended the funeral at St. Patrick's Cathedral, and one of the speakers was Mayor Giuliani. Typical newspaper headline: "Angels Take Wing As 1,600 Say Goodbye."

Nurses are nurses. Advertising executives are advertising executives and are not likely to get the same reception—in life or in death. If four advertising executives had died driving off the Brooklyn Bridge after a three-martini lunch, the media would have treated the story quite differently. "Hucksters Go to Hell in a Honda."

Face reality. In a recent Gallup poll on the honesty and ethics of people in thirty-two different professions, advertising and advertising practitioners ranked near the bottom, right between insurance salesmen and car salesmen. (Shown at left is an abbreviated list with the percentage of respondents who felt people of each profession were honest.)

If you don't believe what an insurance or a car salesman tells you, why would you believe what you read in an advertisement? Both sources have the same degree of credibility.

Not only does advertising have an external problem with the public, but it also has an internal problem.

Advertising's Problem Inside the Corporation

"What strategy does your advertising agency suggest?" we recently asked the CEO of a large client.

"We never ask our agency what to do," he replied. "We tell them."

The advertising era is over. Today clients seldom trust their ad agencies to help them make all-important strategic decisions. What used to be a marketing partnership has degenerated into a client/vendor relationship. (A Patrick Marketing Group study of senior marketing executives found that only 3 percent of those interviewed claimed to have delegated the responsibility for establishing their brand identities to their advertising agencies.)

A recent survey of eighteen hundred business executives by the American Advertising Federation (AAF) shows that public relations is more highly regarded than advertising. The executives were asked which departments were most important to their company's success. Here are the results:

- Product development 29 percent
- Strategic planning 27 percent
- Public relations 16 percent
- Research & development 14 percent
- Financial strategies 14 percent
- Advertising 10 percent
- Legal 3 percent

Only the legal department ranked lower than advertising in the AAF survey. Advertising might account for a substantial share of a company's budget, but in the eyes of management its stature has been seriously eroded.

So what did the AAF do to counter the low score the advertising department received? They did what many companies do when they find themselves in trouble. They launched an advertising campaign to improve advertising's perception in the business community. Theme: "Advertising. The way great brands get to be great brands."

But if you believe that product development, strategic planning, public relations, research and development, and financial strategies are more important than advertising to a company's success (and that is what the survey shows), then why would you believe an advertisement that boldly states, "Advertising is the way great brands get to be great brands"?

It's a classic case of cognitive dissonance. You can't hold advertising in low esteem and also believe an ad that says advertising builds great brands. Except, of course, if you don't believe that great brands are important. Which would mean that the American Advertising Federation now has two problems: advertising *and* brands.

The weakest link in any advertising program is its credibility. An advertising message has little believability with the average person. Advertising is taken for what it is—a biased message paid for by a company with a selfish interest in what the consumer consumes.

Advertising's Golden Era

It wasn't always so. After World War II, advertising was the rising star in corporate America. At Procter & Gamble, Hershey's, Coca-Cola, Campbell's, and many other consumer goods companies, it was the advertising people that ruled the roost.

In Hollywood, they even made movies where advertising people were the heroes. *The Hucksters*, starring Clark Gable and Deborah

Kerr, was a notable example. Also, *The Man in the Gray Flannel Suit* starring Gregory Peck. (People assumed that anyone who wore a gray flannel suit was in the advertising business, but Peck actually played the role of a PR person.)

Helped by the introduction of television after World War II, advertising volume exploded. By 1972, the annual per capita expenditure on advertising was $110. Today, the comparable number is $865. Truly we live in an overcommunicated society and it's not getting any quieter. (Adjusted for the effect of inflation, the 1972 figure would have been $465.)

What happens when the volume of almost anything begins to soar out of sight?

Volume Up, Effectiveness Down

The rise of advertising volume coincided with a decline in advertising effectiveness. Every advertising effectiveness study shows the same results. The more advertising in a given medium, the less effective each individual advertisement is.

An advertisement in a thin magazine will generally be seen and read by more people than an advertisement in a thick issue of the same publication. A commercial on a television show with few commercials will generally be noticed by more people than a commercial on a TV show with many commercials.

Not only has advertising volume risen, but advertising costs have risen even faster. In 1972, for example, the price of a thirty-second Super Bowl commercial was $86,000 and it reached 56,640,000 people. Cost per thousand: $1.52.

Last year a thirty-second Super Bowl commercial cost $2,100,000 and reached 88,465,000 people. Cost per thousand: $23.74 or nearly

16 times as much. (To be fair, if you figure in inflation, the cost today is 3.7 times as much. On the other hand, a 270 percent increase in three decades is a big increase indeed.)

In addition to the media cost, there's also the cost of production which is not cheap either. According to the American Association of Advertising Agencies, the average cost to produce a thirty-second TV commercial is currently $343,000.

Some categories are even more expensive. The average production cost of a thirty-second soft drink or snack commercial is $530,000. For apparel and clothing the average cost jumps to $1,053,000.

If you study advertising rates in all media, you will find exactly the same two trends. Increasing volumes, which reduce effectiveness, combined with increasing costs, which reduce efficiency.

Taken together, these two trends have made advertising an expensive and difficult way to influence customers and prospects. (If you have been thinking that your company was spending more on advertising and enjoying it less, you are probably right.)

Advertising Is an Anomaly

Most products and services go in the opposite direction. As time goes by, prices usually decline.

Compare communicating by phone with communicating by advertising. Back in 1972, the year MCI became operational, the average cost of a long-distance phone call was in the neighborhood of twenty cents a minute. Today it's seven cents a minute or less.

The same phenomenon is true of airline fares, fast food, soft drinks, electronic products, and hundreds of other products and services. Over time as competition develops and as companies learn how to reduce their costs, prices (adjusted for inflation) tend to fall.

In 1990, only 5 million people in the United States used a cellular telephone and their average monthly bill was $81. Today 110 million people use cell phones and their average monthly bill is $45.

In just five years the average price of a digital camera dropped from $560 to $370, at the same time as the number of pixels (a measure of quality) dramatically increased.

Perhaps the best example of constantly declining prices is the computer. A $1,000 personal computer you might buy today is more powerful than the million-dollar mainframe you could have bought thirty years ago.

Advertising Volume Keeps Growing

But higher prices and lower levels of effectiveness have not reduced the volume of advertising. Year after year advertising expenditures outpace the growth in GDP.

In 1997, U.S. advertising expenditures were up 7 percent over the previous year. In 1998, 8 percent. In 1999, 10 percent. And in the year 2000, another 10 percent. (Because of the terrorist attacks, the year 2001 was an exception. Ad spending fell 6 percent, only the second time in the last forty years that advertising spending actually declined from one year to the next.)

Current U.S. advertising expenditures are $244 billion a year, or a record 2.5 percent of the gross domestic product. This is within shouting distance of the Defense Department budget, which was $291 billion in fiscal 2000.

Other countries are beginning to join the United States as advertising-saturated societies. Hong Kong, Portugal, Hungary, Greece, and the Czech Republic already spend a higher percentage of their GDP on advertising than we do. Still, America currently accounts for 44 percent of the world's total advertising expenditures.

237 Messages per Day

How many advertising messages is the average person exposed to during an average day? This is a question many communication experts have tried to answer, with the guesses ranging up to five thousand per day.

But what is a message? Is it a small-space magazine ad or a thirty-second television commercial? How do you compare a page of newspaper ads (with perhaps thirty small-space messages) that a person might be exposed to for half a second with a thirty-second television commercial? Does that mean the person who sees both is exposed to thirty-one advertising messages?

There's a better way to estimate the per-capita daily consumption of advertising. An annual advertising expenditure of $244 billion translates into $2.37 per person per day.

For most people, advertising means television advertising. The average cost of a thirty-second television spot is in the neighborhood of $10 per thousand or one cent per person. Therefore the average person is exposed to 237 television commercials (or their equivalent in other media) every day or 86,500 television commercials a year.

Two hundred and thirty-seven television commercials are a lot of television commercials. It's like watching a full-length motion picture containing nothing but TV commercials. And, of course, "capita" includes everybody from infants to nursing home residents. An upper-income individual in the prime of his or her life can expect to be exposed to four or five times as much advertising.

The Wallpaper Effect

As advertising volume has increased, advertising messages have become wallpaper. Advertisements surround us from early in the morning to late at night. It's not only the volume of advertising that works against its effectiveness, it's also the number of different messages the average individual is exposed to. The New York–based market-research firm CRM, for example, now tracks advertising expenditures for nine hundred thousand different brands.

As a result of the volume and the variety, we tend to tune all advertising messages out. Only when an ad is unusual do we pay any attention to it at all.

Just because an object is large doesn't necessarily mean that anyone will pay attention to it. A typical living room might have 400 square feet of wallpaper, equivalent to 190 pages of the *New York Times*. Yet you can spend several hours in another person's living room without being able to recall a single detail from the paper on the wall.

(If you have wallpaper in your home, when was the last time a stranger walked in and said, "Wow! That's very interesting wallpaper.")

You can be exposed to 190 pages of the *New York Times* advertising with the same result. The inability to recall a single detail from 400 square feet of advertising.

Do you know who Rosario Marin is? How about Mary Ellen Withrow? You don't? That's strange, because you see these names every day on the lefthand side of your money. Mary Ellen Withrow was treasurer of the United States during the Clinton administration; Rosario Marin, during the Bush administration. Money is like wallpaper. Except for the big numbers in the corners, you barely notice what's printed on the bills.

In general, advertising is something you have trained yourself to avoid. If you read all the ads, you wouldn't have time to do anything else.

There are exceptions. Your toilet is overflowing and you look for a plumber in the yellow pages. You're moving to the suburbs and you look for a new house in the classifieds. You're going on a date and you check the movie times in the weekend section.

Save for exceptions like these, perhaps 90 percent of all advertising falls into the "general" category. In other words, it is designed to motivate you to buy a certain brand. This is a difficult task indeed. The average consumer feels that he or she already knows enough about brands in order to decide which brand to buy.

A One-Sided Message

Even more important, the average consumer feels that the information presented in advertisements is one-sided. It doesn't tell the whole story, it doesn't present alternatives, and it is often misleading. No wonder advertising practitioners are only one step above car salesmen.

Who's fooling whom? "Our product contains more vitamins, more minerals, and more proteins, than any other product on the market." Sure, 1 percent more.

"Our truck has the longest wheelbase, the longest cargo bed, and the widest track in the industry." Sure, one inch longer and one inch wider.

Then there's the ever-popular no-nothing claim. "No other battery lasts longer than Duracell." Translation: they're all the same.

Years ago when there was little or no advertising, any advertising was effective. Ads were widely read and discussed. People looked forward to reading the four-color ads in *Life* magazine or watching the commercials on *Texaco Star Theater*.

But you can't live in the past. Advertising is no longer fresh and exciting. There's just too much of it. Advertising has moved to Florida and entered its retirement years.

How can this be when there is more advertising today than there ever was? Both in total volume and in per-capita volume. How can a communications technique be at the height of its popularity and still be on its way out?

History offers an explanation. When a communication technique loses its functional purpose, it turns into an art form.

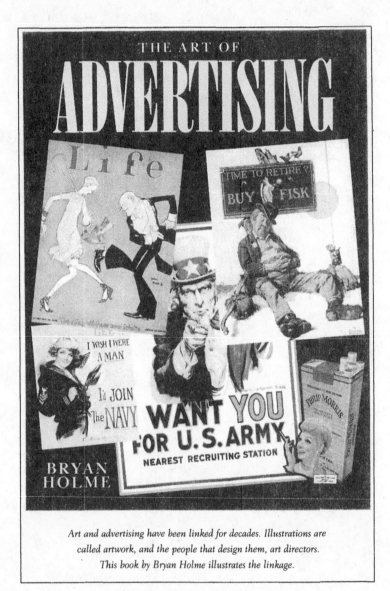

THE ART OF
ADVERTISING

BRYAN
HOLME

*Art and advertising have been linked for decades. Illustrations are
called artwork, and the people that design them, art directors.
This book by Bryan Holme illustrates the linkage.*

2

Advertising *and* Art

Before the age of the printed book, poetry was used to pass along stories from one generation to the next. It's much easier to remember a story in rhyme than one in prose and then retell it to others. Homer (circa 850 B.C.) wrote his masterpieces *The Iliad* and *The Odyssey* in poetry.

Poetry may be just as popular today as it was in Homer's time. The difference is that today poetry is an art form. Its communication function has been lost. Most authors do not use poetry these days to pass along information in verbal form. They use prose because printed books allow text to be easily passed to future generations.

Turning Painting into Art

Before the age of photography, painting was used to communicate the likenesses of kings and queens, princes and princesses, throughout a kingdom. Paintings also let the next generation know what previous generations looked like. Before the age of photography, Rembrandt,

Rubens, Raphael, Michelangelo, Leonardo da Vinci, and other famous artists invariably painted in a realistic style.

(Currently the art world is all shook up by David Hockney's theory that old masters, all the way back to the 1430s, used optical devices to help them produce realistic images.)

Painting is just as popular today as it was in Rembrandt's time. Only today painting is an art form almost totally divorced from reality. As photography gradually assumed the visual communication role, painting turned abstract and became art.

(It's unlikely that you would hang a photograph upside down, but the people at New York's Museum of Modern Art hung Matisse's painting *Le Bateau* upside down for forty-seven days before anyone noticed.)

An inflated price is one of the indicators that a discipline has become an art form. When your great-great-grandfather had his portrait painted for posterity by the local artist, he probably paid for the work by the hour, at a modest hourly rate. Now that painting is an art form, the sky's the limit.

A decade ago *Portrait of Dr. Gachet* by Vincent van Gogh went to a Japanese buyer for $82.5 million. If Dr. Gachet had wanted to let his descendants know what he looked like, he could have had a photograph made and saved someone quite a few dollars.

Art has no function; therefore art has no limit on what it is worth. Art is worth what someone is willing to pay for it. Interestingly enough, that price depends primarily on the publicity a painting has received in the media, not on the amount of advertising run by Sotheby's or Christie's.

Sculpture was once used to create icons or gods. Now that most people no longer believe in stone, brass, or wood gods, sculpture has become an art form. No park in America would be complete without a generous assortment of metal or stone objects, but few people worship them. Sculpture is now art.

Turning Advertising into Art

Like sculpture, painting, and poetry, advertising is taking the same path. "Advertising," said Marshall McLuhan, "is the greatest art form of the twentieth century."

Not only pundits like McLuhan but also top-level advertising people working in the trenches are making the art connection. Mark Fenske, a highly regarded advertising copywriter known for his work on Nike and other brands, says, "It may be the most powerful art form on earth." Advertising legend George Lois entitled his magnum opus *The Art of Advertising: George Lois on Mass Communications.*

Major museums around the world house permanent collections of advertisements. Absolut vodka posters are framed and hung on walls like paintings. An exhibition of Ivory soap ads is on display at the Smithsonian; Coke commercials are in the Library of Congress, and the Museum of Modern Art owns a collection of TV spots.

Television networks put together collections of TV commercials and run them as programming. CBS has *Super Bowl's Greatest Commercials.* ABC has *Best Commercials You've Never Seen (And Some You Have).* PBS has *Super Commercials: A Mental Engineering Special.*

Walk into the offices of virtually any advertising agency in the world and look at the walls. You would think you're in an art museum—wall after wall of advertisements set in impressive mattes and expensively framed.

Hold the phone, you might be thinking. Agencies are just exhibiting samples of their work. Maybe so, but lawyers don't frame copies of their finest briefs. Nor do doctors exhibit pictures of their most brilliant surgeries. We have never visited any advertising agency (and we have visited a lot) and seen framed sales charts for the agency's clients.

What is the role and function of advertising, anyway? Ask any copywriter or art director. Is it to increase the client's sales by 10 percent or is it to win a Gold Lion at Cannes? If they are honest, they will usually admit to going for the gold.

What's wrong with equating advertising with art? Many things, but the fundamental problem is that the creators of such advertising become more concerned with what posterity will think about the work rather than with what prospects will think about the brand.

More and more consumers, too, see advertising as an art form rather than a communication vehicle. How often has someone said to you, "I saw a great TV commercial last night; I nearly fell on the floor laughing."

When you ask them what the name of the product advertised was, they invariably say, "I don't remember." And when they do remember the name of the product advertised, they look hurt if you ask them if they are actually going to buy the brand.

People look at advertising the way they read a novel or watch a television show. They get involved in characters, situations, and plots without the least bit of motivation to act out any of the parts, including buying the product. It's all art. (Some people think that accounting is becoming an art form at companies like Enron.)

Turning the Military into Art

In our society the road between function and art is heavily traveled. Take a typical military function, the changing of the guard.

In Korea, the changing of the guard at 2 A.M. in the morning was a simple ceremony that took about twenty seconds.

"You notice anything, Al?"

"No, except it's colder than hell out here."

"You're relieved. Hit the sack."

At Buckingham Palace, the changing of the guard is an elaborate ceremony that takes twenty minutes or so. Question: What do the guards guard?

Nothing. At Buckingham Palace the changing of the guard has become an art form.

Before the invention of the musket, the sword was an important instrument of war. It's been several centuries since swordplay served any function in warfare.

Has the sword disappeared? Not at all. In the Civil War, every officer carried one. At the courthouse in Appomattox, Lee surrendered to Grant by handing over his sword. Even today, every officer-to-be at West Point has his or her own sword. The sword has lost its function and become an art form.

You can recognize art by its extensive use in everyday language. Even though the sword has no function in today's society, it does live in the language. Nobody says, "Live by the gun, die by the gun."

Turning the Horse into Art

Before the age of the automobile, the horse was the primary means of transportation. Has the horse disappeared with the invention of the automobile? Not at all. Today there are more horses in America than there ever were, but practically none are used for pure transportation. There are horse races, horse jumping shows, and horse riding vacations. The horse has lost its function and become an art form.

More than 7 million Americans are involved in the equine industry, an industry that does $112 billion in business a year. That's bigger than the railway business in America, a functional form of transportation.

Emulating the Art of Painting

The art that advertising people most identify with is painting. Advertising art directors (who are really "layout" or "visual" directors) have modeled many of their campaigns on trends in the field of painting.

- **Minimalism**. Most fashion advertising uses this art approach pioneered by Mark Rothko. A recent eight-page four-color insert in the *New York Times Magazine* used two words in the entire ad. The word *Nautica* on page 1 and the word *Nautica* on page 8.
- **Pop Art.** Many liquor campaigns are modeled on this approach. Called bottle-and-glass advertising, they remind consumers of Andy Warhol's Campbell's soup cans and Brillo boxes. As a matter of fact, one of the most famous Absolut advertisements was done by Mr. Warhol.
- **Abstract Expressionism.** Many supermarket and used-car-dealer advertisements are almost as messy as a Willem de Kooning oil painting. Apparently they want to create the impression that everything is on sale.
- **Surrealism.** Many high-tech campaigns copy Salvador Dalí's approach. The flying men in a recent Microsoft XP commercial are a typical example.
- **Sensationalism.** Many advertising campaigns mimic the work of Damien Hurst, the British artist who cut a pig in half, among his other outrageous acts. The call for entries for the 2001 Atlanta Addy Awards has no copy, just a picture of a blind man with a name tag "Addy judge" following a seeing eye dog.

Getting to Be Famous

Branding in art follows the same principles as branding in marketing. You become a famous artist (or a famous product) by being first in a new category. Over time art critics give the new category a name and associate it with the painter who pioneered the category. Sensationalism and Damien Hurst, for example. Some additional examples:

- Impressionism—Claude Monet
- Pointillism—Georges Seurat
- Expressionism—Vincent van Gogh
- Cloisonnism—Paul Gauguin
- Naive Painting—Henri Rousseau
- Fauvism—Henri Matisse
- Cubism—Pablo Picasso
- De Stijl or Neoplasticism—Piet Mondrian
- Action Painting—Jackson Pollock
- Kinetic Art—Alexander Calder

An artist can't get famous by painting in the style of Picasso. And an automobile can't get famous by being designed in the style of a Porsche. Each is an original. Each is creative in the usual definition of the word.

Which brings up the most overused and under-understood word in the field of marketing.

The current rage in advertising circles is animals.
If you've seen the TV commercials, you know that polar bears
prefer Coca-Cola and lizards prefer Budweiser.

3

Advertising *and* Creativity

If you have ever worked for an advertising agency (as we have), you know that the most overused word in the organization is *creative*.

You have the creative department, the creative directors, the creative approach, the creative strategy, and the creative platform. If it isn't creative, the thinking goes, it doesn't belong in an advertisement or in an advertising agency.

What is an act of creativity anyway? According to the dictionary and according to common uses of the word, creativity is producing something that's original, or new and different.

But what if something "old and similar" works better than something "new and different"? No matter, "old and similar" can't be used because it's not creative. That's what advertising agencies get paid for. Creativity, right?

The Product and Creativity

But doesn't creativity belong in the product rather than in the advertising? Isn't the essence of building a brand creating the perception that the brand was first in some new category rather than creating the perception that the brand's advertising was some sort of breakthrough advertising?

Wouldn't you be less likely to buy a product if you thought the advertising was great and the product mediocre? And more likely to buy a product if you thought the advertising was mediocre and the product was great? And isn't it true that most people think advertising itself is irrelevant and just something to put up with in order to watch television and listen to radio? Or to page through in order to get to the real reading material in newspapers and magazines?

By focusing on creativity, advertising agencies assume that marketing is a battle of advertisements rather than a battle of products. Agencies want to win the advertising war because it means awards, media recognition, and new business.

The Zoo on Madison Avenue

Like artists in search of recognition, advertising people are quick to jump on the latest creative fad. A few years ago, animals were all the rage on Madison Avenue. One of the first advertisers to raid the zoo was Energizer, which did bunnies.

And the animal parade was on. Coca-Cola did polar bears. Budweiser did ants, frogs, ferrets, beavers, and finally lizards. Budweiser's sibling Bud Ice went looking for an animal of its own to sponsor, so they asked themselves, who is most likely to drink an ice beer? You guessed it, penguins. So Bud Ice did penguins.

The Postal Service did eagles. Merrill Lynch did bulls. Taco Bell did Chihuahuas. Allstate did deer. Dreyfus did lions. Yahoo! did dolphins. American Tourister did gorillas. E*Trade did chimpanzees. La-Z-Boy did raccoons. Cadillac did ducks. Range Rover did elephants. BMW did turtles. Turtles? The ultimate driving machine is a turtle? Top speed, two miles a day.

A recent two-page advertisement for the Saturn Vue sport-utility vehicle managed to squeeze in twenty-three different animals.

Are animals in advertising good or bad? Like every question in marketing, the correct answer is always the same: it all depends.

It all depends on what you are promoting. If you are promoting a zoo, animals are probably a good idea. If you are promoting an automobile, probably not.

But the creative mind thinks differently. If nobody else is using animals to promote an automobile, then animals might be a good idea. And to be really creative, the automobile advertising has to incorporate an animal that no one else is using. Hence turtles for BMW.

The zoo parade is likely to continue. More than four thousand species of mammals are available, ranging from the shrew, which weighs seven-hundredths of an ounce, to the whale, which weighs up to 140 tons. The whale, is of course, taken by Pacific Life, but the shrew is still available if you're still interested.

The Search for the New and Different

Al once worked for Renault when they were trying to promote the Renault Dauphine as an alternative to the Volkswagen Beetle. The creative director presented the layout, a one-inch-square photo of the car against a sea of white space on a *Life*-magazine-size page.

"All automobile ads," noted the creative director, "use big pictures of the car. We're going to be different and use small pictures." This is the creative mind at work.

"True," Al replied, "but the Dauphine is a good-looking car and the

Beetle is ugly. It's the only advantage we have. Don't we need a big photograph to demonstrate this advantage?"

Creativity won this battle, as it usually does, and the ads ran as planned. Sales matched the size of the illustrations, and the Dauphine disappeared from the market shortly thereafter.

To feed their creative fires, advertising people often look outside the industry to find new and different ideas. They go to art museums and motion picture theaters, always searching for the unique and different.

Advertising people find movies to be a particularly good source of ideas. Ad agencies often hire filmmakers like Spike Lee, Woody Allen, David Lynch, Errol Morris, the Coen brothers, or Guy Ritchie (aka Madonna's husband) to make TV commercials. When ad agency creative directors want to move up the ladder of life, they often go to Hollywood and make films. (Spike Jonze, Michael Bay, David Fincher, Tarsen Singh, among others.)

The motion picture industry itself is flirting with becoming an art form. An "art film," almost by definition, is a movie that nobody goes to see, and the few people who do see the film don't understand what it's all about.

The Nissan "Toy" Commercial

Many TV commercials borrow ideas from the movie industry. Remember the Nissan "toy" commercial from a few years ago that used Barbie, Ken, and G.I. Joe look-alikes plus the Van Halen song "You Really Got Me"?

Here is how the creative mind creates a commercial like that one. (1) All car commercials use photography, so we will use live-action animation. (2) All car commercials use real cars, so we will use toy cars. (3) All car commercials use real people, so we will use dolls.

Lee Clow, advertising's most celebrated creative director and the mind behind the Nissan spot, summed up his definition of break-through creative work as "advertising that changes the rules in a category. Forever."

Creativity like this really scores with the creative crowd. The spot was named best ad of the year by *USA Today, Time, Rolling Stone*, the International Automotive Show, and a host of other commentators. *Adweek* magazine called the Nissan spot "the most talked-about ad campaign of 1996."

Creativity wins awards, but does it also win sales? The evidence is discouraging. Here is how Nissan and its competitors did in the year the Nissan toy commercial ran. Toyota was up 7 percent. Honda was up 6 percent. The industry was up 3 percent. And Nissan was down 3 percent.

"Nissan's Ad Campaign Was a Hit Everywhere but in the Showrooms" was the headline of a front-page story in the *Wall Street Journal*. The company also took a hit. Nissan Motor Corporation USA cut 450 white-collar jobs, or 18 percent of its white-collar work-force. And Nissan's president left "under pressure" to take a position at Republic Industries.

Meanwhile Nissan's advertising agency drove off with its creative reputation unsullied. Unbelievably, they continue to handle the account today and offer no excuses for the brand's advertising. Clow dismissed the complaints about the lack of effectiveness of Nissan advertising by cavalierly saying, "I don't design the cars." (Nor are you helping sell the cars, Mr. Clow.)

It's like a lawyer who says, "I don't care if my client lost the case, my brief was beautiful."

The Bruce Willis Approach

Advertising has a "wise-guy" reputation. If Hollywood redid *The Hucksters* today, the lead role in the movie would undoubtedly go to Bruce Willis.

A typical print ad for Knob Creek bourbon: "Dad left Johnny the house in the Hamptons and the stables. I got his last case of Knob Creek." Then the punch line: "Dad never did care much for Johnny."

In the advertising world, Johnny got the house in the Hamptons and the stables. In the real world, Johnny would have gotten a nasty lawsuit.

Here are the headlines of some recent wise-guy ads in the automotive field:

- "Rarely do you get to use the words *ingenious* and *muscle-bound* in the same sentence." Chevy Avalanche.
- "May cause avid use of accelerator." Nissan Altima. (Rarely do you get to use the words *avid* and *accelerator* in the same sentence.)
- "As the garage door closes, you think to yourself: Phew, that was fun." Lincoln LS.
- "It's like a monster in a horror movie. It keeps coming back meaner and stronger." Honda CR-V.
- "More upper than crusty." Volkswagen Passat.
- "It's like foie gras at cheeseburger prices." Hyundai.
- "The next thing you know, they'll be putting caviar in trail mix." Jeep Grand Cherokee Overland.
- "It's a big fat juicy cheeseburger in a land of tofu." Dodge Durango.
- "We'll have to keep this introduction brief—the CR-V has plans for the weekend." Honda CR-V.
- "We didn't intend to make other trucks feel pathetic and inadequate, it just sort of happened." Chevy Avalanche.

- "AVS. AHC. VSC. A really bad Scrabble hand or a really good suspension?" Lexus LX 470.
- "Maybe the fountain of youth isn't a fountain at all." Audi A4.
- "Think of it as a four-thousand-pound guardian angel." Jeep Grand Cherokee.
- "Our 270-horsepower engine can beat up your . . . wait, you don't have a 270-horsepower engine." Chevy TrailBlazer.
- "Which style of massage do you prefer: Swedish, shiatsu, Reiki, or Lexus?" Lexus LS 430.
- "The most fun you can have in a car with the seats up." Hyundai Tiburon GT V6.
- "This is beyond feeling the road. This is heavy petting." Acura RSX Type-S.
- "The first car to be insulted by its own price tag." Mitsubishi Lancer.
- "It has a black belt in performance." Nissan SE-R Spec V.
- "It defies everything, including description." Cadillac Escalade EXT.
- "Millions of people are perfectly happy driving boring cars. What makes you so special?" Chevy Impala LS.
- "You are a microscopic speck in the universe. You might as well be a microscopic speck with more power." Chevy Tahoe.
- "Bigger, wider, more luxurious. All of the blah, blah, blah. None of the blah." Chevy TrailBlazer.
- "Raise the bar? It was much more in our character to plow through and cold-cock it in the jaw." Chevy trucks.
- "Some bugs die more noble deaths than others." Dodge trucks.
- "May promote feelings of superiority." Nissan Altima.
- "Explain again why traffic jams are bad." Toyota Camry.
- "So agile it can make a lowercase U-turn." GMC Yukon XL Denali.

Do you remember reading any of these automobile ads? Probably not. Why should you? None of the ads use words that ordinary people use when they are talking about cars. The ads are "creative."

Our "favorite" automobile advertisement demonstrating the excesses of creativity is a full-page newspaper ad for Infiniti. The illustration is a lizard sitting on the steering wheel of an I35. The copy consists of just two sentences:

"There's no greater satisfaction than slipping inside the I35 on a cold day to find a warm steering wheel. As if gripping the wheel of a 255-horsepower sedan wasn't satisfying enough already."

We wonder if a warm steering wheel provides enough motivation to part with $30,000 for an Infinity I35. But many automobile ads contain real innovations buried under wise-guy copy.

Consider an advertisement for the GMC Sierra Denali. "We didn't reinvent the wheel. We just thought all four of them should do the steering." Buried in the copy is the real news: "The world's first and only pickup with four-wheel steering."

Four-wheel steering could be a powerful motivating factor for a truck buyer, but the idea needs the credibility of media coverage. How many vehicles have four-wheel steering? Does four-wheel steering reduce accidents? What do the feds say? Is there any movement to make four-wheel steering mandatory for new vehicles?

Advertising people talk about creativity and the "big idea." But even when an advertisement contains a big idea (and four-wheel steering could be one), the message is usually lost on prospects who don't expect to find such things in advertising.

To be effective, advertising doesn't need creativity. It needs credibility.

ADWEEK

Vol. XXXII No. 25   EASTERN EDITION   June 17, 1991 ● $2.50

CLIO FREE FOR ALL

The Industry's Best Known Show Explodes Into a Frenzy In Which Attendees Raid Stage and Steal Awards

**By Richard Morgan
and Sherrie Shamoon**

NEW YORK—Last week's Clio Awards show turned into a statue-grabbing frenzy. The audience, upset by an improvised presentation that featured the event's caterer as an emcee, finally stormed the stage.

Pandemonium ensued while Clio Awards president Bill Evans made his entry and quick exit almost unnoticed. His last words were that this

The audience, upset by an improvised presentation that featured the event's caterer as an emcee, stormed the stage.

week's show at Lincoln Center, to honor TV, cable and cinema commercials, would go on as planned.

Despite additional assurances from the Clio organization, there are

even more rumors about this week's event than there were about last week's fiasco. Herein is ADWEEK's chronology of the biggest travesty ever to befall the ad-award biz.

Monday, June 10: Rumors about the Clios kicked in with a vengeance at The One Show, held at Lincoln Center. Most of the buzz centered on financial problems, although other reports were as wild as one's imagination.

Wednesday, *(Continued on page 54)*

The universal hunger for advertising awards was demonstrated by the near riot at the 1991 Clio Award show. Attendees rushed the dais and grabbed the Clio statuettes.

4

Advertising *and* Awards

On November 22, 1963, at an annual Art Directors Awards luncheon, the president of the club stood at the podium and said, "President Kennedy has been shot. But I know he would want us to continue."

If you want to get ahead in the agency field, nothing is more important than awards. That's as true for individuals as it is for agencies themselves. The Oscars of advertising are the Gold Lions presented at the International Advertising Festival, held annually in Cannes, France. Win a Gold Lion at Cannes and you will be a king in the advertising jungle.

If you strike out at Cannes, there are always the Andys, the Addys, the Clios, the One Show, the New York Art Directors Club, the Kelly Awards, *Advertising Age*'s Best Awards, and a host of other national and regional award shows. No other industry hands out as many awards as the advertising industry.

Agency bigwigs eagerly await the annual Gunn Report, which uses an intricate point system to log the winners of thirty-one TV and cinema awards shows and twenty print competitions. In all, seventeen countries are included in the report. In 2001 the big winner was Leo Burnett, followed by BBD&O and DDB.

If you're a college professor, the rule is "publish or perish." If you're a creative director, the rule is "win awards or wipe out." (The average advertising agency spends more of its money on award entries than on independent consumer research.)

The pressure to win awards is so great that some agencies enter ads created solely as contest entries. These "fake" ads are a problem for contest administrators around the world. "Ad Competitions Act to Stop Spate of Fake Entries" was the headline of a recent article in the *Wall Street Journal*.

The Milk Mustache

Over the years no advertising campaign has attracted as much attention as the milk mustache "Got milk?" program run by the National Fluid Milk Processor Promotion Board.

Such celebrities as Bill Clinton, Kelsey Grammer, Naomi Campbell, Joan Rivers, Vanna White, Christie Brinkley, Lauren Bacall, Jennifer Aniston, Tony Bennett, Danny DeVito, Venus and Serena Williams, Patrick Ewing, Dennis Franz, and John Elway have been shown with milk mustaches. Just about everybody who is anybody has appeared in the campaign.

As part of pop culture, the campaign has been endlessly lampooned. It has been spoofed, parodied, and copied on everything from *Leno* to *Letterman*, sitcoms to movies, greeting cards to T-shirts. Ballantine Publishing Group even issued a book on the subject, *The Milk Mustache Book* by Jay Schulberg. "A behind-the-scenes look at America's favorite advertising campaign" was the subtitle.

If the milk mustache campaign is American's favorite advertising campaign, why isn't milk America's favorite beverage? Per-capita milk consumption continues to decline, reaching its lowest level ever last year.

Lee Weinblatt, who heads an ad research company, said that

while everyone raves about the milk mustache campaign, milk sales keep going down.

"The main reason why girls don't drink milk is they claim it's fattening. None of the ads address that issue," points out Weinblatt.

Client Thinking

What do clients think of the award mania that affects ad agency moguls? Clients seem to be of two minds.

Middle management loves them. "Hey, somebody thinks our ads are great." And they display the trophies and plaques with as much enthusiasm as their ad agency counterparts. They also find advertising awards helpful in moving up the career ladder, within their own companies or on the outside.

Top management seems to be oblivious to them. We have never heard a CEO say, "Our advertising won an award last year." Either they don't think awards are important or they don't see any connection between winning an award and increasing sales, a connection we fail to see as well.

What we do see in the mind of top management is the increasing realization that advertising has lost its communication function and has become art. No CEO wants to be perceived as a philistine, so he or she tolerates advertising in much the same way that he or she tolerates the expensive annual report, the expensive artwork on the walls of the boardroom, and the Calder mobile on the front lawn. Advertising may not do much good, but it can't do any harm.

Some people think architecture is also on the verge of losing its function and becoming art. Consider the new Guggenheim Museum in Bilbao, Spain. Instead of following Mies van der Rohe (form follows function), many architects today are following Frank O. Gehry (form doesn't matter as long as it's creative and gets attention).

Wherever you look, you see the same pattern. Today's function is tomorrow's art. What you see in a museum might have served a purpose in the past, but it died and became art. A 1911 Mercer Raceabout is a magnificent sight to look at in an automobile museum, but it makes for poor transportation.

Some executives are as proud of their advertising as they are of their corporate art collection. They like it when someone at the country club mentions their latest TV commercial. They like it even better when their advertising slogan becomes a buzzword on the sitcoms and the late-night talk shows.

"The quickest way to make a brand famous," says advertising agency DDB, "is to make its advertising famous. A world that hums your jingle or repeats your catchphrase will feel better about trying your product."

(Note the shift in emphasis from the product to the advertising. We would have thought the idea was to make the product interesting, not the advertising interesting.)

The Budweiser "Whassup?" Campaign

No catchphrase has become as famous as quickly as Budweiser's "Whassup?" The "Whassup?" campaign has won more awards than any other advertising program in advertising history, including the Grand Prix for TV and Cinema at Cannes.

Advertising Age reported the euphoria that erupted when the Cannes award was announced: "The half dozen spots from DDB Worldwide, Chicago, for Anheuser-Busch's Budweiser beer were so widely popular with festival goers that during screening audience members were still shouting the infectious catchphrase two categories after alcoholic drinks ended."

"It was fresh and amusing, and everyone fell in love with it," said one TV judge. "It took about five minutes to decide and was almost one hundred percent."

The following year, Budweiser won a Bronze Lion at Cannes for "What are you doing?" a yuppie spoof of the "Whassup?" campaign. And August Busch IV, Anheuser-Busch's vice president for marketing, was named Advertiser of the Year for the Budweiser campaigns' "outstanding and consistent quality . . . over the past few years."

Wait a minute, did "Whassup?" or "What are you doing?" sell any Budweiser beer? As a matter of fact, U.S. sales of Budweiser beer (in barrels) have fallen every year for the last decade, from 50 million barrels in 1990 to less than 35 million barrels in the year 2000. Whassup, Budweiser?

What is up is Bud Light. Every year for the past decade, Bud Light has increased its sales: from 12 million barrels in 1990 to 32 million barrels in 2000. And in the very near future, Bud Light is sure to pass Budweiser in sales.

Why not give the Grand Prix to the Bud Light advertising? After all, that's the brand that has been increasing its sales. Not to Budweiser advertising, the brand that has been decreasing in sales.

You may not understand the psychology of the creative community. Advertising is art. It has no connection to sales. You contaminate the creative process by introducing commercial considerations.

With one exception, none of the major advertising awards programs considers anything but the ad itself. No advertising objectives, no awareness changes, no sales results, nothing but the effect the advertisement itself has on the judges.

(The one exception is the Effie Awards, presented by the New York chapter of the American Marketing Association. As you might suspect, creative people seldom brag about winning an Effie, short for "effectiveness.")

Maybe Anheuser-Busch is backing Bud Light with more advertising dollars than it is putting behind its core Budweiser brand. Actually the reverse is true. Over the past five years the company has spent 50 percent more on Budweiser advertising than it has on Bud Light advertising.

Sales Value vs. Talk Value

What is the role and function of advertising anyway? You seldom hear the words *selling* or *sales value* when you listen to advertising people talk. According to DDB's chief U.S. creative officer, the real function of advertising is to create "talk value."

The idea is to develop commercials that people chat about at work or use in a punch line at a party. And then, with some luck, the punch line becomes part of the vernacular.

Talk value, a phrase trademarked by DDB, is also called the "Letterman or Leno factor." When creating advertising, DDB copywriters and art directors were told to consider whether the commercial's punch line could make David Letterman's Top 10 list or be used in a Jay Leno monologue.

The Nike "Just Do It" Campaign

Aside from the Budweiser campaign, no advertising has received more talk value than Nike's. "Just do it" has become part of the vernacular of every teenager. And Nike's TV commercials have been very popular.

Currently they feature Vince Carter, Rasheed Wallace, Jason Williams, and other NBA players dribbling a basketball and dancing to pulsating music. Called "hoop-hop" spots, they look more like music videos than TV commercials.

Nike, in fact, managed to air a two-minute version of one of the spots on MTV. So how is Nike itself doing?

Not too well. Four years ago, Nike had 47 percent of the athletic shoe market. Today its market share is down to 37 percent. Nike's stock has fallen from $75 a share in 1997 to $56 today. "Just do it" apparently applies to everything except buying Nike sneakers.

So who is gaining on Nike? Reebok, for one. They did it. They went out and hired Allen Iverson, the hottest young NBA star, to endorse Reebok.

Another is Skechers, the "anti-Nike" brand endorsed by Britney Spears and favored by many teenagers for its irreverent and fashionable image.

The Energizer Bunny Campaign

Another campaign that has generated a lot of talk value is the Energizer Bunny. The Bunny passed the test by making both the Letterman and Leno shows . . . repeatedly. What the Bunny didn't pass is the sales test. Currently Energizer has 29 percent of the U.S. market while Duracell has 38 percent.

Funny thing is, while everyone knows the Bunny, not everybody knows Energizer. Some people think he is the Duracell Bunny. A contestant on one quiz show lost $100,000 making that very mistake. While the advertising campaign is a big success, the brand is a lot less successful.

One of the problems with the Bunny campaign is that Energizer is a No. 2 brand, and "generic" advertising slogans are generally associated with No. 1 brands.

"Just do it" is associated with Nike, the No. 1 brand of athletic shoe. "Whassup?" is associated with Budweiser, the No. 1 brand of beer. So the Bunny is often associated with Duracell.

Fishing Without a Hook

All three slogans, however, share one fatal flaw. They are fishing without a hook. Prospects pick up the bait, but never get hooked on the brand.

- Whassup? "Nothing except I'm thirsty. I think I'll break down and have a Heineken."
- Just do it. "You know you've been wanting that pair of Iverson Reeboks. Just go out and buy them."
- The Bunny died. "We need more batteries. Get another package of Duracell."

Advertising history is littered with popular campaigns that did zilch for the brand. They dangle verbal bait without bothering to add a motivational hook.

- "Yo quiero Taco Bell" and the Chihuahua. (Sales declined and the agency was fired.)
- "The heartbeat of America" for Chevrolet. (Chevrolet lost its leadership to Ford.)
- "There are some things money can't buy. For everything else, there's MasterCard." (MasterCard keeps falling further behind Visa.)

These and hundreds of other advertising slogans are ear candy for the mind. They may be memorable, they may even be connected to the brand in the mind of the prospect, but they don't motivate the public to buy the brand. They are fishing without a hook.

The Alka-Seltzer Campaign

Over the years no advertising has received as much acclaim as the Alka-Seltzer commercials. The newlywed who plans to cook "poached oysters" for her husband. The talking stomach that berates its owner for eating pepperoni pizza. The TV actor who had trouble saying, "Mamma mia, thatsa spicy meatball." The glutton who groans, "I can't believe I ate the whole thing."

Advertising Age selected Alka-Seltzer as the thirteenth best advertising campaign of all time.

Alka-Seltzer's "Mamma mia" spot was voted the funniest television commercial of all time in a survey conducted by MTV Networks.

And where is Alka-Seltzer today? Definitely in need of medication. "Despite some of the greatest commercials in advertising history," said *Forbes* magazine, "speedy Alka-Seltzer is ailing."

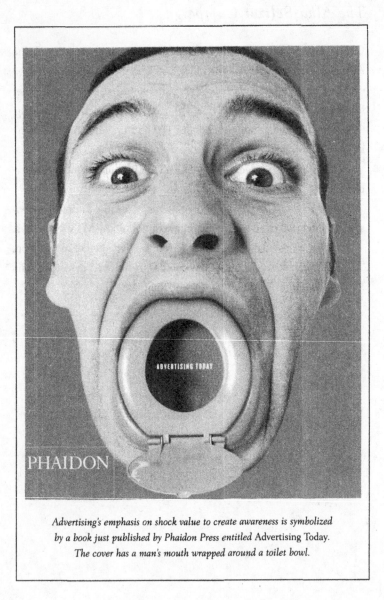

Advertising's emphasis on shock value to create awareness is symbolized by a book just published by Phaidon Press entitled Advertising Today. *The cover has a man's mouth wrapped around a toilet bowl.*

5

Advertising *and* Awareness

It's become an article of faith that one of the primary objectives of an advertising program is to increase brand awareness. And what better way to increase awareness than by running advertising campaigns that attract attention.

"Attention must be paid" seems to be the motto of the advertising crowd. But attention without motivation is a useless attribute. When Volvo drives an automobile into a steel wall, the crash test captures your attention, but it also reinforces Volvo's safety position in your mind. When an advertisement is all attention and no motivation, nothing much is accomplished.

The ad folks go to great lengths to attract your attention. Nissan used dolls. IBM took on a tramp. Pets.com created a sock puppet. Taco Bell employed a Chihuahua. Embassy Suites hired Garfield the cat. Outpost.com rented gerbils to shoot out of a cannon. Xerox dug up Leonardo da Vinci to promote its copier line.

If these were isolated examples of advertising's excesses, it would be one thing. But they're not. Every night you can watch the advertising orgies on network television. (The commercials might be better than the shows, but do they sell you anything?)

Let's look at the awareness issue and the role that attracting attention plays.

Spanning the Brand Spectrum

Look at both ends of the spectrum: brands that no one has heard of and brands that everyone has heard of. Brand recognition seems to follow an inverse bell curve. Most brands are clustered at either one end of the spectrum or the other. The middle is the low point.

Everybody is familiar with Taco Bell. Nobody is familiar with Outpost.com. The same is true of countries. Everybody had heard of Afghanistan. Nobody had heard of Turkmenistan. Try thinking of a country, or a brand, that might have a 50 percent recognition factor. It's not easy.

Ad agencies often justify attention-getting campaigns for low-recognition brands. We have to let prospects know who we are before we can begin to communicate the benefits of doing business with us seems to be the strategy.

But if you have never heard of the company, why would you pay attention to the company's message? You remember the gerbils, but not the outpost. (If you met George Bush at a function last night, you might remember that event for the rest of your life. But if you met George Burke at the same function, you're much more likely to forget him.)

Watching television is exactly the same. You remember the brands you know. You don't remember the brands you don't know. You don't even try to remember the names of the brands you don't know.

It's discouraging. The world's most famous advertising executive once said of our fledgling agency, "They can't be any good if I've never heard of them." You're either famous or you're not; there seems to be no middle ground.

How do you get from one end of the spectrum to the other?

Advertising is an exceedingly difficult way to span the spectrum. Advertising has two strikes against it. Advertising itself has no credibility. And a brand that nobody has ever heard of has no credibility either: "They can't be any good if I've never heard of them."

PR solves both problems. The message has credibility because it comes from a presumably unbiased source. Furthermore, you expect the media to tell you about things you've never heard of. That's what news is all about.

How do we make Turkmenistan famous? Certainly not with advertising.

(Once in a while advertising can turn an unknown brand into a mini-celebrity. The duck campaign for AFLAC is an example. Whether AFLAC will benefit from its advertising is another question. Most people know the duck but not what AFLAC does or what it stands for.)

Let's say your brand is on the other side of the spectrum. Everybody has heard of it. What's the value of an attention-getting advertising program for a brand that everybody has heard of? It's not going to increase your brand recognition, which at 90 or 95 percent is probably as high as it is going to go.

Many ads for brands at the high end of the spectrum are all attention and no message. The Nike "freestyle" or "hoop-hop" spots, for example. What's the purpose of advertising like this? It can't be to increase brand recognition because Nike is already well known.

The Hallmark of Creativity

All attention and no message is the hallmark of "creative" advertising. When you strip away everything that gets in the way of the spot's entertainment value, you create a "pure" piece of advertising art. These are the advertisements that win awards.

The head of the world's most creative advertising agency once lauded a television commercial produced by his agency for Bayless supermarkets. The spot had two scenes.

Scene one, over a roll of toilet paper: "Ladies and gentlemen, bathroom tissue. Right now, for a limited time only, you'll find bathroom tissue on sale at Bayless. And . . ."

Scene two, the same roll with a cardboard tube standing next to it: "Inside every roll of bathroom tissue, you will get a cardboard tube. Absolutely free! [Tag line] The new Bayless."

The spot, which won a Silver Lion at Cannes, proves "once again that big ideas do not depend on big production budgets," said the head of the world's most creative advertising agency.

Funny on the reel, but most likely totally ignored in the living room. Can you imagine anyone watching this TV commercial who might have said, "Let's go to Bayless. They're having a sale on toilet tissue?" We can't.

(It's a spot that only Andy Warhol would have loved.)

You can't defend toilet-tissue advertising on the basis that it makes the supermarket that ran the ad famous. Bayless is already famous in Arizona where its stores are located.

What's the Cause? What's the Effect?

Advertising people often justify attention-getting advertising on the grounds that it makes the product famous. But actually the reverse is true.

The Chihuahua didn't make Taco Bell famous. Taco Bell made the Chihuahua famous. The Bunny didn't make Energizer famous. Energizer made the Bunny famous. The Pillsbury Doughboy didn't make Pillsbury famous. Pillsbury made the Doughboy famous. The

Sock Puppet didn't make Pets.com famous. Pets.com's money made the Sock Puppet famous. Baby Bob didn't make FreeInternet.com famous. FreeInternet.com's money made Baby Bob famous.

What's the cause and what's the effect? Advertising icons seldom cause brands to become famous. But famous brands often cause advertising icons to become famous.

What about brands in the middle with recognition levels among target prospects at roughly 50 percent? Can't advertising push them into the 90 percent range?

Maybe so. But in fact, these midrange brands are going in one direction or the other. Either they have the momentum to move to the high end of the spectrum or they are already on their way down. Advertising isn't needed for a brand moving up and is probably not going to save a brand on its way down.

There are very few half-famous celebrities and there are also very few half-famous brands. Either you are or you aren't.

I want to congratulate Saatchi & Saatchi for starring me in their great Isuzu commercials.

He's lying, it was Della Femina, Travisano & Partners.

What a clever idea! Use a lying car salesman to sell cars. Joe Isuzu became famous, but Isuzu automobiles did not. Sales declined and the agency was eventually fired.

6

Advertising *and* Sales

It used to be called the Curse of Clio. An advertising agency that won a Clio Award for a client was likely to lose that client the following year.

Awarding-winning advertising never seemed to produce the sales increases that clients were counting on.

The Joe Isuzu Story

In spite of the hype that popular advertising campaigns receive, few of them generate sales results to match the hysteria. Who can forget Joe Isuzu, the lying car salesman, from the eighties?

Played by actor David Leisure, Joe hit the airways in July 1986. The following year, Isuzu car sales were up . . . by a minuscule 1.7 percent. From then on, it was all downhill.

In 1988, Isuzu car sales were down 38 percent. In 1989, they were down 34 percent over the previous year. In 1990, they were down 64 percent over the previous year.

In 1991, American Isuzu Motors fired the agency that had created the Joe Isuzu campaign. In 1992, Isuzu announced it would stop production of passenger cars.

And so it goes. The advertising operation was successful but the patient died.

Many advertising people rationalize Isuzu's relative lack of success by citing the notoriety created by the campaign. Even though Joe Isuzu was a car salesman, maybe his notoriety helped sell Isuzu trucks. But look at the numbers. The year Joe Isuzu arrived on the scene was the high-water mark for Isuzu vehicle sales (both cars and trucks) in the United States. Total 1986 sales: 127,630.

Never again would Isuzu sell that many vehicles in the U.S. Current sales are less than 100,000 a year. Now what do you suppose American Isuzu Motors is doing about this situation? You're right. They're bringing back Joe Isuzu.

"With sales lagging and its image sagging," writes Bruce Horovitz in the *Chicago Sun-Times*, "American Isuzu Motors is returning to one of the most memorable of all ad icons."

With Joe Isuzu's track record, why would the company rehire him? It makes no sense, but it does show how traditional advertising thinking dominates the marketing community.

The goal of traditional advertising is to not to make the product famous. The goal of traditional advertising is to make the advertising famous. Instead of creating sales value, traditional advertising attempts to create talk value.

Joe Isuzu is amusing, but in real life why would you buy a car from a lying car salesman? Why would you buy a car from a car company who uses a lying car salesman on television? Where is the motivation? All bait and no hook.

The Parity Product Argument

Another excuse for putting Joe Isuzu on television is the "parity product" argument. In mature categories, such as beer, automobiles, and athletic shoes, goes the thinking, all brands are the same. They're parity products or commodities. Traditionally, advertising for these parity products has aimed not to inform—what is there to say?—but to entertain.

This line of thinking permeates the creative corridors of many advertising agencies. Creative people are quick to see "parity products" in almost any category they work on. It's another excuse to do entertaining ads by people who would rather be making movies than making ads anyway.

There's a hole in parity product thinking. While many products might be quite similar, there are few parity product perceptions.

Bud Light and Miller Lite beer might be parity products in the bottle, but they are definitely not parity products in the mind. Bud Light is the "with-it" beer for the younger crowd. Miller Lite is the "has-been" beer for the older crowd.

Marketing doesn't deal with products. Marketing deals with perceptions. To run a successful advertising or public relations program, you have to create a lot more than talk value. You have to deal with those nasty perceptions in the prospect's mind.

Publicity or PR is a more effective way to deal with those perceptions than advertising.

Some of the blame for advertising's failure to move the needle can be laid to hubris, the notion that no matter what the marketing problem is, the answer is always "more advertising."

The story is told of a client with a number of serious problems. The company's production facilities were outmoded, the product was priced too high, and customers were turning to competitive brands.

"What should we do?" the client asks the CEO of its advertising agency.

The CEO's response: "I'd recommend network television."

If the only tool in your toolbox is a hammer, every problem looks like a nail. Why should things be different if you run an advertising agency?

If quality (spelled creativity) doesn't work in advertising, maybe quantity does. Maybe by increasing the volume of its advertising a company can find success. Let's look at how some of the largest advertisers have fared recently.

The Chevrolet Story

For a number of years, the largest advertised brand in America was Chevrolet. Last year, General Motors spent $819,200,000 advertising its Chevrolet brand, 67 percent of that on television.

What did General Motors get for its $819 million? Is Chevrolet the largest-selling automobile brand? No, it's not. Ford is. Is Chevrolet the largest-selling truck brand? No, it's not. Ford is.

As a matter of fact, General Motors spent 39 percent more advertising its Chevrolet brand than Ford Motor Company did advertising its Ford brand. Yet Ford outsells Chevrolet by 33 percent.

Well, you might be thinking, the folks at Chevrolet wouldn't be spending that money if the advertising program wasn't working. (And our government wouldn't be spending $20 billion a year on farm subsidies either if that program wasn't working.)

This is not a one-year phenomenon. For five years in a row, Chevrolet has been out-advertising and under-selling Ford.

Five years ago, Ford sold 28 percent more vehicles than Chevrolet. Then the Chevrolet advertising blitz began. In five years, Chevrolet spent $3.4 billion on advertising compared to $2.9 billion for Ford.

Just because you out-advertise your competition doesn't mean you are going to outsell them. Today Ford has increased its lead over Chevrolet from 28 percent to 33 percent.

An even more striking comparison is in the cost of advertising per vehicle sold. In the current year Chevrolet is spending $314 per vehicle sold compared to $170 for Ford.

Now what would you do if you ran the Chevrolet Division of General Motors? Increase your advertising budget or reduce it?

The AT&T Story

The brand that received the second-largest advertising budget last year was AT&T. The AT&T brand was backed by $711 million in advertising. So how is AT&T doing? Not well at all.

A stumbling communications company, AT&T is seeking to sell its telephone operations to one of its Baby Bell offspring. And it plans to merge its cable service with Comcast.

According to the *New York Times*, "For AT&T, the effort to sell its telephone operations, which include the largest consumer long-distance company, is yet another sign of the way a groping business strategy and a protracted long-distance price war have left the company a battered shell of its former self."

Maybe, just maybe, AT&T also has a groping advertising strategy.

The General Motors Story

Forget individual brands such as AT&T and Chevrolet. Look at General Motors as a whole. In 1994, Ronald Zarrella joined GM from Bausch & Lomb as its marketing chief. His mandate: bring the discipline of brand management to the world's largest corporation.

General Motors' new marketing chief, according to *USA Today*, was going to smash to bits the old auto industry belief that "product is king." Ron Zarrella said that GM's future depended as much on good marketing as good products: "There's a belief in this industry that product is everything—and it's not."

True to his brand-management roots, one of the first things that Mr. Zarrella did was to turn up the advertising turbocharger.

- In 1995, General Motors was the third-largest advertiser in America, spending $2.1 billion.
- In 1996, General Motors was the second-largest advertiser in America, spending $2.4 billion.
- In 1997, General Motors was the largest advertiser in America, spending $3.1 billion.
- In 1998, 1999, and 2000, General Motors was again the largest advertiser in America, spending $3.0 billion, $4.1 billion, and $3.0 billion, respectively.

So what did General Motors get for all this money?

- In 1995, General Motors' market share dropped from 34.0 percent to 33.9 percent.
- In 1996, General Motors' market share dropped to 32.3 percent.
- In 1997, General Motors' market share dropped to 32.1 percent.
- In 1998, General Motors' market share dropped to 30.0 percent.
- In 1999, General Motors' market share dropped to 29.6 percent.
- In 2000, General Motors' market share dropped to 28.1 percent.

By the time Ron Zarrella left GM in 2001 and returned to Bausch & Lomb, his thinking had come full circle. "Product is everything in this business," he said.

It's strange. Advertising is not everything and product is not everything, but there is one thing that is everything. And most managers seem to miss it.

Perception is everything. The only question is how to create a favorable perception in the consumer's mind. And advertising has racked up a poor track record in this respect.

Wal-Mart vs. Kmart

More often than not, big advertising budgets are associated with companies with big problems. Compare Wal-Mart with Kmart. Who spends the most on advertising?

Would you believe Kmart does? Last year Kmart spent $542 million on U.S. advertising and Wal-Mart spent $498 million.

When you compare revenues, however, it's a different story. Last year Kmart had domestic revenues of $37 billion, compared to Wal-Mart's $159 billion, more than four times as much.

Now that Kmart is bankrupt, what would you do to turn the retailer around? Increase your advertising expenditures?

Inside Wal-Mart, the anti-advertising story gets even more interesting. One of Wal-Mart's operations is Sam's Club, a division that does virtually no advertising. While the average Wal-Mart store does $46 million in annual sales, the average Sam's Club store does $56 million in annual sales.

It's hard to make a case for advertising when most of the big advertising spenders have problems and most of the small advertising spenders do not.

Advertising expenditures are often like legal expenditures. Both can be negative indicators. A company with big legal bills is not necessarily a company on the way up.

The Target Story

Another discount chain that's a heavy advertiser is Target. Unlike Kmart, however, Target has benefited from a heavy dose of favorable publicity. Oprah Winfrey has referred to the stores in faux French as "Tarzhay." Sales are soaring and the chain is very profitable.

Target has fed the publicity fires by hiring architect Michael Graves to design a collection of housewares and home decor items. They also bought out clothing designer Mossimo and retained him to design a line of clothing. And Target stocks some hot brands such as Calphalon kitchenware.

Customers refer to the store as "cheap chic." Whether it's the advertising or the PR (and the word of mouth) that is driving Target's success is an open question. Our vote is the PR.

(As with many marketing programs today, there's a disconnect between the advertising and the customer perception. Target's advertising focuses on visual symbolism using the "target" logotype, while the targets of Target's advertising, its customers, talk about wide aisles, neat displays, and hip merchandise. No one ever says, "I go there because they have this neat trademark.")

The Sears Roebuck Story

Another big advertising spender in trouble is Sears, Roebuck. Last year Sears spent $1.5 billion on advertising for its catalog of brands, roughly three times as much as either Wal-Mart, Kmart, or Target. Yet domestic revenues of Sears were smaller than even Kmart's.

There are, however, a lot of fringe benefits in being a big advertiser. Marketing and advertising managers get treated like high rollers in Las Vegas. Meals, entertainment, you name it. At Super Bowl time, the NFL throws a party for several thousand of its advertisers and hangers-on in keeping with its position as the highest-priced advertising buy. After attending an NFL Super Bowl extravaganza, you can actually feel bad if you bought only one $2 million spot.

In advertising, as in Vegas, there are plenty of players, but few winners. If the advertising industry had an annual convention in Newport, Rhode Island, one might be tempted to ask, "Where are the big advertisers' yachts?"

General Motors vs. General Electric

Take another comparison: General Motors versus General Electric. General Motors is No. 3 on the Fortune 500 list and General Electric is No. 5.

When it comes to advertising, General Motors is the bigger spender. The $3.0 billion that GM spent on U.S. advertising last year was almost two and a half times the $1.3 billion spent by GE.

Big advertising spenders are not generally big moneymakers. General Motors, even though its sales were 42 percent higher than GE's, netted only $4.5 billion on sales compared to $12.7 billion for General Electric.

Big advertising spenders are not generally worth as much on the stock market either. General Motors, the bigger spender, has a market capitalization of $27 billion, while General Electric, the smaller spender, has a market capitalization of $405 billion, fifteen times as much.

Compare the two Jacks. John F. Smith Jr., chairman of General Motors, and John F. Welch Jr., former chairman and CEO of General Electric.

Jack Welch is the toast of the business community, perhaps the most famous CEO in America. His book, *Jack: Straight from the Gut*, received a $7 million advance and went straight to the top of the best-seller lists.

Jack Smith, chairman of General Motors, is as anonymous as his name.

The Coca-Cola Story

At Coca-Cola, a longtime pillar of the advertising establishment, things are not going well with advertising. The company has been changing management, advertising agencies, and advertising campaigns with some regularity.

KO, the stock market symbol for Coca-Cola, has not been a knockout on the market. Since CEO Roberto Goizueta died in 1997, the market value of the company has declined from $145 billion to about $119 billion today.

Over the past five years, Coca-Cola's advertising has suffered from a double whammy. No buzz and no fizz. Nobody talks about Coke's advertising (the buzz), and the advertising contains no motivation to buy the product (the fizz).

For a function that is supposed to be customer-oriented, advertising people are surprisingly insular. One columnist, perhaps the most famous advertising critic in the world writing for the most famous advertising publication in the world, called a recent Coca-Cola slogan the greatest tag line in soft-drink history, maybe in marketing history.

Come on now. "Always" is the greatest tag line in marketing history? Have you ever heard anyone say, "Give me an Always?" Or, "I'll have a rum and an Always?" And what does "always" mean anyway? That customers always drink Coca-Cola?

The truth is quite the opposite. If they run out of Coca-Cola, 99 percent of all cola drinkers would be happy to accept a Pepsi-Cola. That's the reality.

Coca-Cola has drifted from one meaningless advertising slogan to the next. From "Always" to "Enjoy" to "Life tastes good." In July 2001, Coca-Cola suffered the embarrassment of having to pay almost $1 million to Parmalat Canada because it had infringed on the same "Life tastes good" slogan used by Parmalat on its Lactantia butter brand.

Then two months later, in the aftermath of the terrorist attacks, Coca-Cola dropped "Life tastes good" altogether.

In many ways, advertising is a lose/lose game. If your slogan is meaningless (as most slogans are), it doesn't help the brand. If your slogan is meaningful, it isn't believed by the prospect.

This is advertising's Achilles' heel. Just because you say something meaningful and motivating in an advertisement doesn't necessarily mean the prospect will believe what you say.

The McDonald's Story

Take McDonald's, the brand with the fourth-largest advertising expenditure. In the past five years, McDonald's spent over $3 billion on U.S. advertising.

McDonald's sales, however, haven't kept up with inflation. During the same period, the average per unit sales at McDonald's inched up from $1.4 million to $1.5 million, an increase of just 1.7 percent a year. Advertising isn't doing much to move the Big Macs at McDonald's.

Recently, McDonald's CEO Jack Greenberg told a franchisee convention that "marketing was broken" and the company was working to fix it.

But advertising's biggest failure in recent years has nothing to do with big companies and their big advertising budgets. It has to do with small companies in an emerging market.

*Many dotcoms tried to establish brands with hefty advertising budgets,
including Pets.com. "Because pets can't drive" was the theme,
but sales were dismal and the site was folded.*

7

Advertising *and* *the* Dotcoms

The Internet boom in the late 1990s created a major problem for many dotcom start-ups. With everyone jumping on the Net, how could any single site generate enough publicity to build name recognition?

To solve the problem, many Internet companies turned to advertising. Since we can't get publicity for our dotcom, went the thinking, we'll launch the site with a big advertising program.

Why Buy Pet Supplies at Pets.com?

Pets.com was a Web site selling pet supplies to dog and cat owners. Hardly an exciting PR idea. So naturally Pets.com called on the advertising community for help.

Pets.com hired a marketing manager from Procter & Gamble and an advertising agency with the best creative reputation in the business. True to its roots, the agency created the Sock Puppet, which *Advertising Age* called the "first bona fide advertising celebrity to be created in dotcom land."

The Sock Puppet was a smashing success. It won awards and

kudos from consumers, the media, the trade press, and marketing experts. The Sock Puppet marched in Macy's Thanksgiving Day parade, appeared on CNN and *Good Morning America*, and was profiled in *Entertainment Weekly, Time,* and *People*. Recently an original Sock Puppet was auctioned off to a San Francisco businessman for $20,100.

The only thing missing in this fairy tale was sales. In little over six months, Pets.com spent more than three times as much on marketing as its $22 million in revenues. With that kind of fiscal track record it didn't take long for Pets.com to bite the dust and go bankrupt.

What didn't die was the agency's faith in advertising. "Business models, market conditions, the Nasdaq, VCs—they're not in my control," said the president of Pets.com's advertising agency. "This has nothing to do with the success of the advertising. Ad agencies are hired to create brands, and we did that in spades."

We did that in spades? We created a successful brand? What is a brand anyway? The president of the world's most creative agency is confusing the advertising with the product. The Sock Puppet is not the brand. (If it were, the Web site would have been selling sock puppets.) Pets.com is the brand.

A brand is a name that stands for something positive in the prospect's mind. Volvo stands for "safety." BMW stands for "driving." But what did Pets.com stand for? A brand without a positive position in the mind is a brand that won't motivate consumers to buy anything. Furthermore, most pet owners had trouble figuring out whether the Sock Puppet belonged to Pets.com, Petstore.com, or Petopia.com.

Why should I buy my pet supplies at Pets.com? The company needed to answer that question first and then try to put the answer inside the pet owner's mind. Not an easy job and not a job that advertising handles very well. The ad agency's answer was that you should shop at Pets.com "because pets can't drive."

Ridiculous, of course, but that's advertising creativity at work.

Why Buy Books at Amazon.com?

When Amazon.com started in business, it had a simple answer to that question: "All hardcover books for 30 percent off." And publicity, not advertising, helped to communicate Amazon's 30-percent-off idea.

Sure, after the Amazon.com brand was established, the company did run a major advertising program. But it wasn't advertising that built the brand, it was PR. The advertising only reinforced the brand position already established by the PR.

Internet cemeteries are filled with brands that tried to reverse this process—that tried to use massive advertising to become well-known without first using PR to build the company's credentials.

The eToys Tragedy

Another high-profile dotcom dud was eToys. Founded in 1997, eToys was soon spending as much as 60 percent of its revenues on advertising. The company went public in May 1999, reaching a first-day market valuation of $7.7 billion, 35 percent greater than its brick-and-mortar rival Toys "R" Us. In the Christmas season that year eToys spent $20 million on an elaborate advertising program.

Fifteen months later the company was bankrupt. Once worth billions, eToys received only about $10 million for its inventory, equipment, furniture, fixtures, trademark, and Web address.

Another toy retailer that tried to use advertising to build an Internet brand was Toysmart. Toysmart.com lasted just 482 days, even though it sold a controlling stake to the Walt Disney Company for around $50 million. It used part of the money to finance a $21 million ad campaign touting "good toys."

This was way too early to launch an ad campaign. The Toysmart

Web site would have needed years of publicity, or perhaps decades, to establish itself as the only place that refused to sell toys of a destructive nature or the latest fad, à la Pokémon. This kind of message needs the wholehearted support of the media if it is going to be used to build a brand.

The Value America Disaster

Value America, the Internet department store, was another dotcom that tried to use advertising to buy its way into the mind. Launched in October 1997, the Web site had big plans. At the end of the year its founder boasted that ValueAmerica.com would be spending $150 million on advertising in the next eighteen months.

Six months later Value America was running full-page advertisements in the *Wall Street Journal,* the *New York Times,* and *USA Today* and also advertising in trade publications, on radio, and even on TV in most major markets. In 1999 alone the Web site spent about $60 million on advertising. That year Value America generated $183 million in sales and a loss of $144 million.

Putting big bucks behind a weak name is a deadly combination. It will work only when you have a monopoly. Where there is real competition, you need the most appropriate name you can find and then you need to conserve your advertising resources until you can establish your credibility.

At the end of 1999 new management took over at Value America. The first task was to come up with a new logo, a new Web site design, and a new name. ValueAmerica.com was going to become VA.com (it didn't seem to matter that VA.com suggested the Veterans Administration or the state of Virginia).

By August of 2000, the company was bankrupt.

Other Dotbomb Disasters

You may not remember the heavy emphasis that dotcom companies put on advertising to help them build their brands. Two-thirds of all the commercials aired during the Super Bowl of 2000 were dotcom advertisements.

In a single year (2000) Art.com spent $18 million on advertising. AutoConnect.com spent $15 million. CarsDirect.com spent $30 million. Drugstore.com spent $30 million. Homestore.com spent $20 million. Living.com spent $20 million. Petstore.com spent $10 million. RealEstate.com spent $13 million. Rx.com spent $13 million.

Do you remember any of this dotcom advertising? Do you remember any of these dotcoms?

"Last year's dotcom advertising burst did colossal damage to advertising's reputation among the nation's CEOs," wrote Rance Crain, editor-in-chief of *Advertising Age*. "The dotcom advertising was so pointless, so stupid, so tasteless, that it shook the faith of corporate chieftains in the power of advertising for their own brands."

What was the dotcom problem? Pointless, stupid, and tasteless advertising? Or maybe the problem was depending on advertising to build a brand when they should have been using PR.

One of the biggest problems with Value America's "big bang" advertising launch was its lack of flexibility. With a slow start nourished by publicity, you can make changes as you go along. In spite of a Web site that sold everything including office supplies, books, pet supplies, apparel, specialty foods, automobiles, and consumer electronics, roughly 85 percent of Value America's revenues came from computers and software. Value America needed a name more like CompUSA.

(The future is unpredictable. We once talked with an entrepreneur in the United Kingdom who had started a chain of used-book stores. His sales, he figured, would be 80 percent fiction and 20 percent nonfiction. His numbers turned out to be exactly right, only the categories were reversed. It was 80 percent nonfiction and 20 percent fiction.)

Wal-Mart vs. Value America

Contrast Wal-Mart, the world's largest retailer, with Value America. Sam Walton opened his first Wal-Mart discount store in Rogers, Arkansas, in 1962. Eight years later Wal-Mart went public with eighteen stores and sales of just $44 million.

In those eight years Sam Walton generated reams of publicity for his Wal-Mart stores but spent little on advertising. Only after the publicity had made Wal-Mart a household name could the company spend its advertising dollars efficiently.

It's not question of a fast start (Value America) versus a slow start (Wal-Mart). A company should start as fast as the publicity allows it to start. You can't jump-start the process.

Could Value America have become successful by emulating Wal-Mart's slow-start strategy? Probably not. Where's the PR angle? Here was a Web site that attempted to sell everything from hot tubs to hot-chocolate mix, from toothbrushes to high-end TV sets. Unlike Amazon's simple message, hardcover books for 30 percent off, Value America had no message that merited publicity coverage. It was just another Internet site trying to sell everything.

If you want to launch a new brand today, you need a message that gets media attention. Without publicity your new brand will fail no matter how good the product or how good the service. It's not enough to have a better product or service. You need a better PR idea.

Sometimes even a better PR idea is not enough. In its short life-time, Webvan, the grocery-delivery Web site, generated enormous publicity, 99 percent of which was favorable.

But how could any company make money selling groceries at supermarket prices and then throwing in free delivery? A dumb idea backed by great PR is still a dumb idea with no future.

We once did strategy work for two Internet companies that violated the fundamental principle of PR first, advertising second. Both were backed by big companies with deep pockets. And both were marketing disasters.

The WingspanBank.com Wipeout

The first client was WingspanBank.com, which was launched in June 1999 with a flurry of newspaper, radio, and television advertising.

Don't run advertising, we warned, until you have established the bank's credibility in the media. Notwithstanding our warnings, the bank spent $100 to $150 million launching the site, according to press reports at the time.

Not a good idea. Of all services, a bank needs consumer confidence if it is going to be successful. You might take a chance on a restaurant or a dry cleaner, but not on a bank.

"Bank One Corporation, conceding that its highly touted WingspanBank.com was a failure," reported the *Wall Street Journal*, "plans to fold the two-year-old Internet-only bank into the rest of its on-line banking operations."

Too bad. There is still an opportunity to establish an Internet-only bank with lower service charges and higher rates on savings, but it can't be done with advertising. It can only be done with PR.

The HomePortfolio.com Downfall

The second client was HomePortfolio.com. After a day of consulting, including our standard recommendation to start the program with PR, the two founders seemed anxious to leave. Sure enough, a few weeks later we noticed full-page newspaper and magazine ads promoting the site.

Fifteen months later HomePortfolio.com closed its retail operations and transformed itself into a software supplier for the on-line furnishings market. This was not a shoestring operation. HomePortfolio.com received well over $50 million in financing.

In our opinion both WingspanBank and HomePortfolio were excellent ideas killed by advertising-oriented thinking. As marketing consultants, we can't discuss our specific recommendations, but you can be sure they relied primarily on PR. You have to win the PR battle first before you can launch an advertising war.

How do you win the PR battle?

You set up a new category in the mind you can be first in. Then make sure the new category has a motivating factor that will encourage prospects to switch from the old category to the new.

This is easy to say, but difficult to do. The science of marketing works against the notion of setting up a new category. The first question normally asked by a marketing practitioner is "What's the size of the market?"

For a new category, the size of the market is zero.

The Garden.com Collapse

Take Garden.com, another Web site that blossomed, withered, and died around the same time as HomePortfolio.com did. What's the size of the gardening market?

Gardening, it turns out, is America's most popular hobby. It's a $47-billion-a-year industry, about twice the size of the book business. If Garden.com could get just 5 percent of the gardening market, it would have annual revenues of $2.3 billion, bigger than Amazon.com's book business.

With numbers like these, it was no surprise that Garden.com attracted $106 million in venture financing. All to no avail. In November 2000, the site was shut down. The unanswered question: Why should I buy my gardening supplies at Garden.com?

It's a widely accepted belief that these and many other dotcoms were done in by terrible advertising. But that doesn't make sense. Why would an advertising agency say to itself, "It's a dotcom, let's do a ditsy ad"?

A more likely scenario is that dotcom advertising was no better or no worse than advertising in general. But because dotcoms were new brands, advertising was a totally inappropriate vehicle.

Dotcoms That Have Done Well

While many dotcoms have died, others are alive and well and prospering. The successful sites were all first in a new category combined with a powerful motivating factor that generated plenty of favorable publicity.

- **America Online** wasn't the first Internet service provider, but it was the first ISP to get into the prospect's mind, thanks to a generous helping of PR. Furthermore, on December 1, 1996, AOL introduced a flat-rate service, a strong motivating factor. (Initially the service was priced at $19.95 a month. Currently the service is $23.90 a month.)

- **Amazon** wasn't the first Internet bookstore (Powells.com was), but Amazon was first to get into the prospect's mind. And it had the 30 percent discount as the powerful motivating factor.

- **Monster** was probably not the first job search site on the Internet, but it was first to get into the prospect's mind. Furthermore, the 800,000 jobs listed on the site is a strong motivating factor.
- **EBay** was the first on-line auction site. With 29 million registered users and millions of items offered, eBay's motivating factor is its size and strength.
- **Priceline** was the first on-line "bidding" site for airline tickets and hotel rooms. Its motivating factor is the substantial savings that can be achieved by using the site.
- **Travelocity** and **Expedia** weren't the first on-line travel sites, but they were the first sites to get into the prospect's mind. Their motivating factors are the price and itinerary comparisons found on the sites.

What's the size of the market? That's not the best question to start with when you're looking for a new category to be first in.

The question to start with is, what new category can we create? Does that new category have any publicity value? And what angle can we use to motivate prospects to prefer this new category?

The problem with appealing to an existing market is that the market is already taken. The cola market, the beer market, the vodka market, are all enormous markets, but they are already claimed by such brands as Coca-Cola, Budweiser, and Smirnoff.

When you do find a new category to be first in and a powerful motivating factor, you can be sure that the advertising crowd is going to show up and offer to help. That's when you have to keep advertising's key liability clearly in mind.

Making It Right.

You have our word on that.

When you buy tires, you're not just buying rubber and steel... you want the confidence that your tires will get you to your destination—safely. Your safety is our primary concern. We want you to have confidence in the way Firestone tires are made and the way they perform. We'll do whatever it takes, however long it takes, to gain your trust.

We call this our *"Making It Right"* plan. With your satisfaction as our goal, Firestone is expanding warranties and making important enhancements in manufacturing and quality control. In the role of watchdogs, a new team of top technical and quality control managers has been assembled to continuously analyze tire and safety data. They'll act to uncover issues *before* they become problems. We believe in our tires. We want to prove to you that you can believe in them as well. *We'll make it right. It's that simple.*

Inflate.
Rotate.
Evaluate.

How to maintain your tires

Maintaining your tires, including checking air pressure monthly, helps protect them from damage and extends the mileage. Most important, properly inflated tires help ensure the security of you and your family on the road. This free brochure will give you the simple steps to tire safety. Get your copy by visiting our web site or your nearest Firestone retailer.

John Lampe,
CEO, Firestone.

CHECK YOUR
AIR PRESSURE
MONTHLY

Firestone
America's Tire Since 1900
www.firestonetire.com

tiresafety.com

Advertising doesn't have the credibility to counteract unfavorable
publicity. Tire buyers didn't believe Firestone when the
company claimed it was "making it right."

8

Advertising *and* Credibility

The local diner that advertises "finest in food" on its marquee has a credibility problem. The billion-dollar corporation that spends $2 million on a Super Bowl spot has exactly the same problem, although it might not recognize it.

Exaggerated claims and excessive volumes are contributing factors to the decline in advertising's effectiveness, but credibility is the fundamental issue. No matter how creative the advertising, no matter how appropriate the medium, there is just no way around the issue of credibility.

An advertising message is perceived to be one-sided, biased, selfish, and company-oriented rather than consumer-oriented. Ask yourself, do you believe what you read in advertisements? Most people don't. As a result, most people don't read advertisements or pay much attention to radio and television commercials either.

Actually it's worse than that. In a certain sense, every advertising message implies the opposite of what the advertiser intended. In some situations, this "implication of the opposite" is so strong that the advertising can actually harm rather than help the advertiser.

Let's say a seafood company runs an ad that says, "Tests show

Super Seafood is absolutely safe to eat." What would a reader think?

"People must have gotten sick eating Super Seafood, otherwise they wouldn't have run an ad like that."

Making It Right

Who ran this ad: "Making it right. You have our word on that. When you buy tires, you're not just buying rubber and steel . . . you want the confidence that your tires will get you to your destination—safely. Your safety is our primary concern"?

It wasn't Goodyear, Goodrich, or Michelin. They don't need to run advertisements on tire safety. The public has no reason to believe that their tires are unsafe.

It was Firestone that ran the "Making it right" advertising campaign. But you already knew that because of the extensive publicity.

"Tread Failures Lead to Recall of 6.5 Million Firestone Tires," said the headline of an article in the *New York Times*. "Facing 50 lawsuits, 46 deaths, 80 injuries, and a federal investigation, the company said it would provide free replacements for the 6.5 million tires still on the road."

The naïveté that pervades the advertising community is enormous. After fifty lawsuits, forty-six deaths, eighty injuries, and a federal investigation, we're going to solve Firestone's problems by running an advertising program that says don't worry about the safety of Firestone tires because we're "making it right"?

The implication of the Firestone advertising, of course, is just the opposite. "They must be worried about the safety of Firestone tires, otherwise they wouldn't be running a multimillion-dollar ad campaign on the subject."

Quality Is Job 1

For over a decade, Ford has been saying, "Quality is Job 1." Do customers believe that Ford makes better-quality cars than its competitors? Research says no. Among the big carmakers, Ford ranks lowest in terms of quality.

In fourteen different car and truck categories, according to the latest J. D. Power & Associates survey, not a single Ford brand was in the top spot on "initial quality." In the same survey, the Ford brand was rated below average in "customer service." Nor did the Ford brand make the top ten in "sales satisfaction."

The message (quality) might be right, but the messenger (advertising) is wrong. Advertising has no credibility. Advertising is not believable because consumers perceive it to be biased. Advertising is the voice of the seller. To the prospective buyer, advertising has no objectivity. There's no way for a consumer to independently verify the accuracy of what an advertisement claims.

There have been so many outrageous advertising claims that most people consider all advertising "puffery." The usual defense in a legal case involving exaggerated advertising claims is to label them "normal advertising puffery."

Your Safety Is Our Top Priority

When it came to the Explorer rollover problem, Ford was just as naive as Firestone. The company ran advertising that said, "Your safety is our top priority. You have my personal guarantee that no one at Ford will rest until every recalled tire is replaced." The ads were signed by Jacques Nasser, president and CEO of the Ford Motor Company. (Mr. Nasser himself was recently replaced.)

What should Ford and Firestone have done?

Nothing. The only hope they have is that over time tire buyers will forget. And they will, if Firestone waits long enough. Time heals all wounds. Running ads in this situation is like throwing gasoline on the fire. It aggravates the problem by reminding tire buyers that the company has safety problems.

When an airline loses a plane, it immediately cancels all advertising, usually for at least a month. It certainly doesn't run ads saying, "We're redoubling our maintenance efforts."

The Implication of the Opposite

Not only CEOs, but celebrities, movie stars, and politicians often fail to consider the connotations of what they say. When Richard Nixon, the only president of the United States ever to resign, said, "I will not resign," everyone in America knew he would.

And what do you suppose people thought when Nixon said, "I am not a crook"? Exactly.

And what do you suppose people thought when George Bush Sr. said, "Read my lips, no new taxes"? Exactly.

And what do you suppose people thought when Bill Clinton said, "I did not have sexual relations with that woman . . . Monica Lewinsky"? Exactly.

And what do you suppose the financial community thought when President Fernando de la Rua reassured the world that Argentina would not default on its debts? Exactly. (And they were right.)

What are the implications of running an ad that says, "Big sale. Everything in our store 50 percent off"?

Exactly. People will think you rip off customers because your regular prices are way too high.

The Implications of Advertising

What are the implications of running airline advertising that promises big savings if you book two weeks in advance and stay over Saturday night?

Exactly. People think airlines rip off their customers by charging regular fares that are much too high.

What do you suppose car buyers thought when Oldsmobile ran an advertising campaign that said, "This is not your father's Oldsmobile"?

Exactly. They wouldn't be saying that if old people weren't driving Oldsmobiles. "I don't want to drive the same car my father drives." Sales dropped 15 percent.

The Oldsmobile campaign had everything a good advertising campaign was supposed to have. It was a creative success, it had talk value, it became part of popular culture. It did everything except sell cars.

What do you think of King Fahd of Saudi Arabia? The Saudis have been spending millions on an advertising campaign designed to bolster his reputation, including twelve-page four-color ads in the newsweeklies.

Cover quote from George Bush Sr.: "An extraordinarily cooperative, determined, principled monarch. He's a wonderful man. I have known him personally. I have known him in a most respectful way."

What do you think of King Fahd? Most people think he's a totalitarian leader of a dictatorial state. Will the twelve-page ads change that perception? We doubt it.

What happens when you meet someone you haven't seen in a dozen years and he or she says, "You look great"?

Exactly. You think to yourself, I must look awful.

And what do you suppose management people thought when the

chairman of the American Association of Advertising Agencies said, "More and more clients are losing faith in the most fundamental principles of our business: run good advertising, sell more stuff, build better brands, make more profits."

Exactly. Advertising must be in trouble.

The Four A's chairman added this thought: "Advertising is not being seen for what I think it is—the single most powerful tool to produce profitable sales growth and to increase brand value, which in turn should further dramatically improve client profitability."

Read my lips: Advertising is the single most powerful tool to produce profitable sales growth and to increase brand value.

Exactly. Advertising must really be in trouble.

When advertising people tout the value of advertising, they fall into the same trap that advertising itself has fallen into. Their words imply the opposite.

"Advertising is in trouble. We have to reassure our customers that advertising is still their most powerful brand-building tool."

But advertising is in trouble in the boardrooms of corporate America. Which is exactly why the leaders of the Four A's make speeches on the subject and why the American Advertising Federation is running its "great brands" campaign.

You know advertising is in trouble when the advertisements themselves brag about it. The current series of Nextel TV commercials featuring Dennis Franz, who plays Detective Andy Sipowicz on *NYPD Blue*, is a good example.

"I don't do commercials," Mr. Franz hollers into his Nextel phone. "They're dishonest. They lie. I'm supposed to peddle some product I don't even use? Forget about it, I'm not going to do it." (The only clue that this is a Nextel ad is a TV screen on the kitchen counter that plays a Nextel commercial in the background.)

Another sign that advertising is in deep trouble is the shift of funds from advertising to promotional activities (both consumer and trade). In packaged goods, a longtime advertising bastion, advertising's percentage of the marketing budget fell from 60 percent in 1977 to about 30 percent today.

Then there is the pressure to find alternative media.

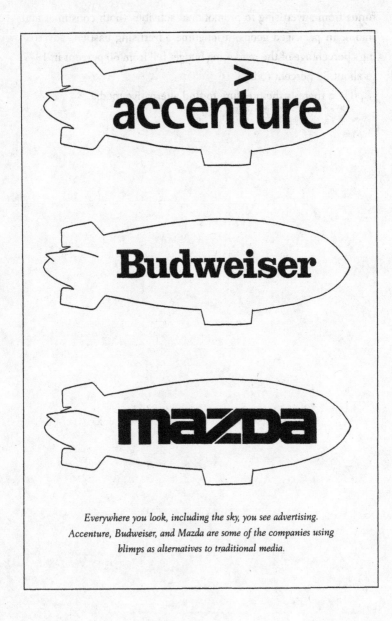

Everywhere you look, including the sky, you see advertising.
Accenture, Budweiser, and Mazda are some of the companies using
blimps as alternatives to traditional media.

9

The Search *for* Alternatives

Another sign that traditional advertising is in trouble is the intense interest in alternative media. Clients are thinking outside the print and broadcast box and coming up with some weird and wonderful ways to spend their advertising dollars.

Blimps are a current favorite. Pioneered by Goodyear and MetLife, advertising blimps are now being used by many companies. Accenture, Budweiser, CDW Computer Centers, Horizon Blue Cross/Blue Shield, Hood, Monster.com, Izod, Mazda, and Sanyo are just some of the companies currently flying blimps.

For about $3 million a year, your company can put its message on an aerial billboard. Advertising blimps are not just a U.S. phenomenon. Companies around the world are using them, including Fagor in Spain, Liebherr in Germany, and StarHub in Singapore.

In addition to flying an advertising blimp over a sports stadium, you can also put your name on the stadium itself. Here are some recent deals, the sports teams involved, the durations, and the prices:

- Adelphia Coliseum, Tennessee Titans, 15 years, $30 million
- CMGI Field, New England Patriots, 15 years, $115 million

- Compaq Center, San Jose Sharks, 15 years, $49 million
- Enron Field, Houston Astros, 30 years, $100 million (Recently the Astros paid $2.1 million to void this stadium deal.)
- Ericsson Stadium, Carolina Panthers, 10 years, $20 million
- FedEx Field, Washington Redskins, 20 years, $205 million
- Heinz Field, Pittsburgh Steelers, 20 years, $457 million
- Invesco Field, Denver Broncos, 20 years, $120 million
- MCI Center, Washington Wizards, 20 years, $44 million
- Pacific Bell Park, San Francisco Giants, 24 years, $50 million
- Philips Arena, Atlanta Hawks, 20 years, $200 million
- PSINet Stadium, Baltimore Ravens, 20 years, $105 million (When PSINet went bankrupt, the Ravens bought back the naming rights for $5.9 million.)
- Qualcomm Stadium, San Diego Chargers, 20 years, $18 million
- Reliant Stadium, Houston Texans, 30 years, $300 million
- Safeco Field, Seattle Mariners, 20 years, $80 million
- Savvis Center, St. Louis Blues, 20 years, $72 million
- Staples Center, LA Lakers, 20 years, $100 million

If you don't want to buy the whole stadium, for a hefty fee you can put your corporate name on the game itself. Currently we have the AXA Liberty Bowl, Capital One Citrus Bowl, Chick-fil-A Peach Bowl, Culligan Holiday Bowl, FedEx Orange Bowl, SBC Cotton Bowl, and the Tostitos Fiesta Bowl, among others.

The logical next step is to name the team. Federal Express reportedly offered to pay as much as $120 million to call the new NBA team in its hometown the Memphis Express. Naturally they wanted to attire the team in the FedEx colors, orange and purple. The NBA said no, but corporate names on sports teams are bound to come. Ironically the National Basketball Association's original Fort Wayne franchise, the Pistons, now in Detroit, was named for the Zollner Piston company.

Then there are "team doctors." Some medical groups are paying as much as $1.5 million a year to be the health-care sponsor of a major-league baseball team. Twenty-five clubs have health-care sponsors. Five have exclusive agreements.

Team sports seem headed in the same direction as individual sports like NASCAR, where both the cars and the drivers carry an advertising load that boggles the mind. A single race car might carry twenty logotypes of its sponsors. And the first thing a driver does upon winning a race is to grab the sponsor's drink, the sponsor's sunglasses, and the sponsor's hat before exiting the car.

In the future, you may see race-car-type advertising on the roads. A new technique called vehicle wrapping allows a colorful vinyl advertisement to be wrapped around an ordinary car. Advertisers like General Mills and Procter & Gamble are paying people something like $250 a month to drive their advertising-wrapped cars around cities.

Wherever you drive today, you can't escape the clutches of advertising. More and more gasoline pumps and ATM machines are carrying advertising messages.

Even your local mall might be available for sponsorship. Discover Mills, a new mall outside Atlanta, is sponsored by the Discover credit card.

Then there is "in-tunnel" advertising, an offbeat and fast-growing phenomenon that began in Europe. Adidas and Coca-Cola bought space in the subways of Budapest and Athens through MotionPoster, an English company. The company has contracts to install in-tunnel systems in Frankfurt, Munich, and Seoul.

In-tunnel advertising uses a series of illuminated signs that, when seen from a speeding train, appear to be animated. The effect, similar to that of a flip book, is not unlike watching a thirty-second television commercial.

You Can't Escape Advertising

Advertising messages bombard us everywhere we go. You can't escape on an airplane. In-flight television programs are loaded with ads. Even airline ticket folders contain advertising messages. The current AirTran folder has nine pages of advertising. Monster.com even carved its corporate logo into a five-acre field under the glide path of Chicago's O'Hare airport.

You can't escape at the supermarket. In addition to displays, posters, and shelf coupon dispensers, you often find advertising printed on the back of your receipts.

You can't escape in an elevator. More and more high-rise office buildings are replacing money-losing Muzak with moneymaking video ads.

You can't escape in a bathroom. Many clubs and restaurants have advertisements on the inside doors of the stalls. At the California State Fair, Procter & Gamble is "Charminizing" rest rooms to illustrate the tangible benefits of its paper products.

You can't escape at the beach. A New Jersey company, Beach 'n Billboard, will imprint your ad on sand. For $20,000 or so, you can get half a mile of beach ads every day for a month.

In the future you may not be able to escape in a book. Italian jeweler Bulgari commissioned best-selling author Fay Weldon to write a novel called *The Bulgari Connection*. The book's cover has a picture of a Bulgari necklace that plays a key role in the plot.

"So-called ambient advertising is exploding," states *Time* magazine, "as companies eschew traditional mass media in an attempt to get at jaded consumers where they work, shop, and play."

Advertisers are winning starring roles in new television shows, painting their messages on concrete barriers in parking spaces and seeking permission to insert products electronically into TV reruns as they currently do on many baseball TV broadcasts. They are also paying to place their products in motion pictures.

For about $4 million, Honda is sponsoring *Pulse: A Stomp Odyssey*, a large-format film shot for IMAX theaters. Pfizer also sponsored an IMAX film on behalf of its Certs brand.

Why are so many advertisers looking for alternative media? The simple fact is that traditional advertising isn't working very well. If it were, you wouldn't see blimp, beach, bathroom, or book advertising.

It's not enough to have a better product or service. It's not enough to have a better price. To be successful today you need to create a better brand. And what is a brand? A brand is a perception in the prospect's mind.

Perception is the name of the game, and advertising is perceived as the only way to create a better perception. Not true, but that's the perception.

There Is a Better Alternative

And that better alternative is publicity or, as its practitioners like to call it, PR, or public relations.

Whatever you call the function (publicity, PR, or public relations), the objective is the same. Tell your story indirectly through third-party outlets, primarily the media.

There are many disadvantages to PR. You can't control the content, you can't control the timing, and you can't control the visual appearance of your message. You can't even be sure that any of your messages will be delivered.

But the one advantage of PR makes up for all of its disadvantages. PR has credibility, advertising does not. People believe what they read in newspapers or magazines or what they hear on radio or see on television.

Customers are cynical, suspicious, and cautious. As the volume of advertising escalates, they are turning to independent, third-party, authoritative sources for recommendations and advice. Friends, relatives, neighbors, and of course, the media in all of its diversity.

Seldom do they check the ads.

PART TWO

The Rise of PR

*PlayStation became the largest selling video-game brand thanks
primarily to media endorsements such as this cover article on
PlayStation 2 in the March 6, 2000, issue of* Newsweek.

10

The Power *of a* Third Party

"All I know," said Will Rogers, "is just what I read in the papers." It's true. Most people only "know" what they read, see, or hear in the media or what they learn from people they trust.

Life is complicated. Who has the time to independently check the quality or features of the wide variety of products and services that one might want to purchase? We let ourselves be led around by the media.

Who makes the "best" automobiles? Ask the average person this question and you'll often get the answer Mercedes-Benz. Then ask, Do you own one? No. Have you ever driven one? No. Do you know anyone who owns one? No.

They how do you know who makes the best automobiles? You have to be a humorist like Will Rogers or Jerry Seinfeld to admit the obvious. "All I know is just what I read in the papers."

Most people determine what is best by finding out what other people think is best. And the two major sources for making that determination are the media and word of mouth.

You can't live in a modern world observing reality with just your own eyes and ears. You have to depend on the eyes and ears of third-party sources that stand between you and reality. Media outlets are the vital links that add meaning to most lives.

Without the information supplied by the media, you couldn't participate in the political or economic life of a capitalist society. You may not believe everything you read in the papers, but you are enormously influenced by the media.

Compared to the power of the press, advertising has almost zero credibility. Suppose you were offered a choice. You can run an advertisement in our newspaper or magazine or we'll run your story as an article. How many companies would prefer an ad to an article?

No one. Advertising has no credibility.

Some companies have even taken to running advertisements that look like editorial content. But this subversive tactic is quickly blocked by publishers, who label the page with the dreaded word *advertisement*. This single word greatly undercuts both the readership of the message and its credibility.

Be honest. How do you read a newspaper or magazine or watch a television show? Don't you differentiate between the editorial and the advertising? Don't you only look at ads that you find exceptionally interesting or amusing? And even then, don't you view the advertiser's message with a great deal of skepticism?

A typical newspaper is 30 percent editorial and 70 percent advertising. What do you spend most of your time reading? To the average person the editorial stories are islands of objectivity in a sea of prejudice.

Advertising's Dirty Little Secret

Regis McKenna, the well-known marketing consultant, writing in the *Harvard Business Review* more than a decade ago, put it this way: "We are witnessing the obsolescence of advertising. . . . First, advertising overkill has started to ricochet back on advertising itself. . . . The second development in advertising's decline is an outgrowth of the first: as advertising has proliferated and become more obnoxiously insistent, consumers have gotten fed up. The more advertising seeks to intrude, the more people try to shut it out. . . . The underlying reason behind both of these factors is advertising's dirty little secret: it serves no useful purpose."

Microsoft reportedly spent $1 billion in advertising for the worldwide launch of Windows XP. But what will motivate prospects to switch from Windows 98, Windows Me, or Windows 2000 to Windows XP? Certainly not what they read in the advertising. They will make their decisions based on the thousands of publicity stories that have run in the media.

"Oracle will run your Web," says a full-page advertisement in the *Wall Street Journal*, "3 times faster than IBM or Microsoft." What do you suppose the average reader thought when he or she read this Oracle message?

"There must be a gimmick." And what do you suppose the average reader thought when the Oracle ad added, "Or we will give you $1,000,000."

"Now, I know there's a gimmick. Larry Ellison doesn't give away a million dollars except perhaps to himself."

Suppose it's true. Suppose Oracle will run your Web three times faster than IBM or Microsoft and there are no gimmicks. Would you still believe the Oracle ad?

When evaluating messages like the Oracle one, readers always look for the loophole. And the last loophole is always, "How come I didn't read about it in the editorial pages? Surely someone would write a story if Oracle's claim and offer was actually legitimate."

For a print advertisement or a radio/TV commercial to be effective, it generally needs outside validation. The message has to be one that the prospect has heard about in the media itself.

Do As I Say, Not As I Do

It's ironic that America's advertising agencies, the "advertising builds brands" crowd, do almost no advertising themselves. Rather they depend heavily on PR to build their own brands. They deluge the trade press, especially *Advertising Age* and *Adweek*, with samples of their work. No award, no matter how trivial, goes uncrowed.

We looked through five consecutive issues of *Advertising Age*, and except for a few classified help-wanted ads, we couldn't find a single advertisement from an advertising agency.

"Do as I say, not as I do" seems to be the motto of the agency establishment. They sell advertising to others, but they don't buy any advertising for themselves.

In addition to the trade press, ad agencies vigorously seek publicity for themselves and their advertising in the big five: the *Wall Street Journal*, the *New York Times*, *USA Today*, the *Los Angeles Times*, and the *Chicago Tribune*. Publicity is the name of the advertising agency game today.

How can you believe in advertising for others if you don't believe in advertising for yourself? Advertising: the way great brands get to be great brands, except for advertising agency brands.

Maybe professional service firms like advertising agencies don't need to advertise. Maybe their reputations suffice to bring them all the business they need. This might be true, but ad agencies have no trouble recommending big advertising budgets for professional service firms like PricewaterhouseCoopers, KPMG, Deloitte & Touche, Ernst & Young, and Arthur Andersen.

(Will the advertising program run by Arthur Anderson save the firm? Don't count on it.)

Advertising for PR Purposes

Many agencies also develop client advertising campaigns whose sole purpose is to generate publicity, not to sell anything. The best example is the Apple Macintosh commercial "1984," which ran only once during the 1984 Super Bowl program.

Tell the truth. If you had seen the Macintosh TV commercial (as one of the 237 messages that assaulted you on that particular Sunday), would you have remembered it a day later? A week later? A year later?

People remember that TV commercial today because of the many stories that appeared in the media. The publicity made the advertising memorable. Without the PR, the Macintosh spot would have been just another television commercial.

(By the way, if the Macintosh advertising was so effective, how come the Macintosh brand is not up there with market leaders Dell, Compaq, Hewlett-Packard, and IBM?)

Agencies like advertising that generates publicity because the publicity benefits the agency as much as the client. At many agencies the ads are merely the hooks on which to hang a publicity campaign.

Perhaps the most effective publicity-generating ad campaign of all time was a 1984 series of Pepsi-Cola commercials starring Michael Jackson. Pepsi had the good fortune to have Jackson's hair catch on fire during the shooting of one of its commercials, and the press went wild. The publicity generated by the hair fire benefited Pepsi-Cola much more than any of the TV commercials did.

Three years later, Coca-Cola came back with Max Headroom, who for a short time became a minor celebrity featured on the cover of *Newsweek* and in other media outlets.

The advertising industry has pretty much given up on what used to be called "salesmanship in print." This was the notion that an advertisement was a surrogate salesman who would tell prospects about the features and benefits of the brand. You can't blame them. Advertising today has so little credibility that it just isn't an effective salesperson.

What's replacing salesmanship are the twin goals of talk value/publicity value. Agencies want to create campaigns that spark both word of mouth and word of media. And their prime weapon for doing so is shock value.

Applying Shock Therapy

If people won't pay attention to the benefits of buying the brand, ad people conclude, then the only recourse is to apply shock treatment. Animals, celebrities, seminudity, sexual innuendo, violence, anything to capture the viewer's attention and especially the attention of ad columnists like Stuart Elliott at the *New York Times* and Bob Garfield at *Advertising Age*.

No one has played the shock game better than Benetton, the Italian clothing retailer. A priest kissing a nun, a dying AIDS victim, a prison inmate on death row, a black stallion mounting a white mare, a newborn baby with its umbilical cord still intact . . . these are just some of the shocking visuals that have appeared under the United Colors of Benetton banner. The ads have made the campaign creator, Oliviero Toscani, world famous. (While Benetton has been successful in Europe, the company has had problems in the United States.)

Actually Benetton has an interesting PR idea that it has never fully exploited. Benetton makes most of its garments in neutral colors that can quickly be dyed to match demand. (Hence the slogan United Colors of Benetton.) A PR-oriented marketing program might have been a more effective (and less expensive) way of establishing the Benetton brand.

Altoids, an Exception to the Rule

Let's be realistic, though. Some products do not have much publicity potential. Take peppermints, for example. The longtime category leader Tic Tac has been overthrown by Altoids, "the curiously strong mints."

Could a PR-oriented marketing program have done the job? Probably not. There isn't much publicity potential in a $2 tin of peppermints. Rather, Altoids used sampling and print advertising to do the job. Some Altoids ad headlines: "The mints with the kung fu grip." "Not recommended for the faint of tongue." "Mints so strong they come in a metal box."

Interesting enough, the Altoids campaign used none of the elements that have become de rigueur on Madison Avenue. No animals, no celebrities, no seminudity, so sexual innuendo. Altoids just went back to basics: create a new category (strong mints) you can be first in. Then give the prospect a reason (curiously strong) for buying the product.

Even though the Altoids brand was not built by publicity, the success of the brand has generated a fair amount of media attention. Success and publicity are so intertwined today, it's hard to find one without the other.

The Reminder, Not the Argument

An advertisement cannot be the argument. It can only be the reminder.

This reminder function can be important, but only after a brand has established its credibility in other ways, generally by public relations. (See chapter 21, "Maintaining the Brand.")

Advertising as a brand-building tool is dead. But advertising has a second life as a brand-maintenance tool, once the brand has been built by PR.

The way to build a brand is with public relations.

Founded 1886.

Microsoft

Founded 1975.

These are the two most valuable brands in the world.
Advertising may have built the Coca-Cola brand, but not
the Microsoft brand. Most people can't remember
a single Microsoft ad.

11

Building *a* New Brand *with* PR

What's the most reported company in the world? According to Carma, a media analysis company, the most reported company in the world is Microsoft.

Microsoft is only twenty-seven years old, yet the Microsoft brand has become the second most valuable brand in the world, just behind Coca-Cola. According to Interbrand, the brand valuation company, the Microsoft brand is worth $65 billion.

A marketing mantra, repeated endlessly by advertising mullahs, is that advertising builds brands. And great advertising builds great brands. Did advertising build the Microsoft brand?

No, a thousand times, no. If Microsoft had not run a single advertisement or television commercial in its twenty-seven-year lifetime, does anyone doubt that Microsoft would still be the world's second most valuable brand? We don't.

Size Doesn't Build Brands

You might be thinking that publicity didn't build the Microsoft brand either. Microsoft is a powerful brand because Bill Gates built a big successful company called Microsoft. Does the power of a brand lie in its size and not in its publicity?

Not in our opinion. Have you ever heard of Cardinal Health, Delphi Automotive, Ingram Micro, Lehman Brothers Holdings, McKesson HBOC, Reliant Energy, Southern, Tosco, TIAA-CREF, or Utilicorp United?

Each of these ten companies is bigger than Microsoft, but none of them have built a brand that compares with mighty Microsoft. Take TIAA-CREF, for example. Last year the company had $38 billion in revenues compared to Microsoft's $23 billion. But Microsoft is a brand. TIAA-CREF is a joke.

Publicity Builds Brands

Massive amounts of publicity built the Microsoft brand. We're quite sure you can remember reading dozens of stories about Microsoft and Microsoft products. Windows 95/98/NT/2000/XP, Word, Excel, PowerPoint, Xbox, .Net. But do you remember a single Microsoft ad? What was the headline? What did the ad tell you? Especially, what did the ad tell you about Microsoft that you didn't already know?

What about the successful launch of the Windows 95 brand? you might be thinking. Do you really think it was the $200 million Microsoft spent on advertising and promotions that made Windows 95 a success? Or the $8 million Microsoft paid the Rolling Stones for the rights to their song "Start Me Up" for the television commercials?

Was it "Start Me Up" that made people line up outside stores for hours waiting for the midnight release of Windows 95? No. Windows 95 would have been a success with no advertising at all. It was the revolutionary product, the media's relentless coverage of it, and their conclusion that 95 would be the future of PC computing that catapulted 95 to superstardom.

To introduce Windows XP, Microsoft paid Madonna a small fortune for her song "Ray of Light." But the success of XP lies in the hands of the media, not in the hands of Microsoft and its advertising campaign. People will be swayed one way or another by the publicity, not by the melodious voice of Madonna.

In building brands, advertising has become irrelevant. What builds brands are media messages. The more messages, the more favorable the messages, the stronger the brand.

Note, too, that publicity built Bill Gates into one of American's best-known corporate executives. It obviously wasn't advertising that elevated Gates into a powerful personal brand name.

Building the Linux Brand

One of the best examples of how publicity can build a brand is Linux. Here is a brand that has never had any advertising because it's not owned by anyone. Linux is "open source" software freely available to programmers, who can view the underlying source code and modify it to meet their needs.

As a brand, Linux has some 99 percent recognition in the high-tech community, and it has made its creator, Linus Torvalds, world famous. You know the brand is famous when the chief executive (Steve Ballmer) of its chief competitor (Microsoft) attacks the brand as "a cancer that attaches itself in an intellectual-property sense to everything it touches."

(Every brand needs an enemy; it's one of the enduring principles of marketing. Pepsi-Cola has Coca-Cola. Burger King has McDonald's. The Republicans have the Democrats.)

There are a number of so-called nongovernmental organizations that have managed to build powerful worldwide brands with PR techniques only. They include Greenpeace, the World Wildlife Fund, PETA, and Amnesty International.

Building the Segway Brand

Is it possible to build a well known brand in a short period of time with no advertising at all? Sure. The launch of the Segway superscooter illustrates the key elements in a brand-building program using nothing but PR techniques.

1. *The slow buildup*. It's absolutely essential to leak information to the media in order to build interest and suspense in the product before it is actually launched. Under the code name "ginger," the Segway superscooter was the subject of many stories in the media and on the Internet for almost a year before its December 2001 announcement. The frenzy began in January 2000 when it was reported that a $250,000 contract had been signed by the author of a book detailing his new, but still secret, creation. Excerpts from the book proposal, published on Inside.com, only heightened the mystery.

2. *A new category name*. The media only wants to print what is new, not what is better. One of the most important decisions you need to make is what to call your new category. The Segway was called a "human transporter." This category name will never stick. With the exception of pipelines and boxcars, all transportation devices carry humans. A better name, in our opinion, would have been "gyro scooter."

3. *A new brand name.* When it comes to picking a name, most companies make one of two mistakes. They either choose a line extension name (Kodak digital cameras), which undermines the importance of the new category, or they choose a generic brand name (Fun Saver cameras), which undermines the importance of the brand. Segway is neither. It stands alone as a brand name. (Razor superscooter would have been a line extension name. Gyro scooter would have been a generic name.)

4. *A spokesperson with credentials.* Dean Kamen, the brains behind the Segway, is a scientist and highly successful inventor. Among other things, he created the iBot, an all-terrain wheelchair that can climb stairs; the intervascular heart stent used to reduce blockages in arteries (recently used in Dick Cheney's heart procedure); a portable dialysis machine; and a drug infusion pump.

When the Segway was finally launched, the media went ballistic. Dean Kamen started the day on ABC's *Good Morning America*, and did interview after interview on the product. The Segway was featured on CNN, *NBC Nightly News, CBS Evening News, ABC World News Tonight*, and most local news stations. On the Internet, the Segway was in the top four of the most popular search items, just behind Christmas, Xbox, and Harry Potter. And there were big Segway stories in virtually every daily newspaper in the country.

Segway and Microsoft are high-tech, you might be thinking. What about low-tech? If advertising doesn't build high-tech brands, advertising might have an important role to play in building low-tech brands.

Building the Red Bull Brand

Red Bull is about as low-tech a brand as you can find. Introduced in Austria in 1987 as the first energy drink, Red Bull is a lightly carbonated, highly caffeinated concoction containing liberal quantities of herbs, B-complex vitamins, and amino acids.

With virtually no advertising, but with liberal amounts of PR and merchandising, Red Bull has become a worldwide success and made Dietrich Mateschitz, the founder of the company, the richest man in Austria. Worldwide sales of Red Bull last year were $895 million.

One thing that drove the publicity was that Red Bull was initially forbidden in Germany because of the high doses of some of its ingredients. As a result every German teenager wanted to try it. (Even today some people believe that the Red Bull sold in Germany is not the real thing.)

Mateschitz based his drink on Krating Daeng, a popular health tonic he had encountered in Thailand. All of which proves you don't have to invent something to get rich and famous. All you have to do is to recognize a potentially good idea, invent a new category and a new brand name, and get them into the mind first.

The success of Red Bull waved a red flag in the face of America's soft drink conglomerates. To counter the Austrian threat, they launched energy drinks of their own. Some of the brands include Adrenaline Rush, Anheuser-Busch's 180, AriZona Extreme Energy, Blue Ox, Bomba Energy, Dark Dog, Deezel, Energade, Energy Fuel, Go Fast, Go-Go Energy, Hansen's Energy, Hemp Soda, Hype, Jones Energy, Magic, NRG Plus, Power Horse USA, Red Alert, Rx Extreme, and XTO.

In spite of a host of competitors, Red Bull has 70 percent of the U.S. energy drink market. And it's highly unlikely to lose its leadership position in the foreseeable future.

Building the Zara Brand

The fastest growing fashion brand in the world is Zara, a Spanish clothing retailer. Except for biannual storewide sales, Zara does no advertising at all. Yet Zara did $1.2 billion in sales last year from more than five hundred stores in thirty countries. (Zara is opening new outlets, on average, once a week.) So far only a few outlets are open in the United States.

Like Red Bull, Zara started slowly. It took thirteen years for Inditex (Zara's parent company) to open the first Zara store outside of Spain. Like Red Bull, Zara has a unique idea. Zara was the first retail fashion chain to adopt a "just-in-time" strategy. Instead of the typical nine months it takes a fashion brand to go from design to delivery, Zara short-circuits the process to fifteen days or less.

Furthermore, Zara doesn't overstock, reducing the need for the frequent and massive sales typical of department store chains. Production is in small batches. If an item doesn't sell, production is halted. Each week 35 percent of the merchandise in a typical store is changed.

Zara's revolutionary concept has created favorable publicity and loyal customers. On average, a Zara customer visits a Zara shop 17 times a year versus 3.5 times for other fashion chains. (Some Spanish women have stopped buying fashion magazines. They just go to Zara to see what's new.)

Amancio Ortega, the reclusive entrepreneur who owns Zara (and a number of other retail concepts, including Massimo Dutti, Pull & Bear, Bershka, Stradivarius, and Oysho), is reportedly the richest man in Spain, with a net worth of $6.6 billion.

Advertising Is No Substitute for PR

The "King of Colas" recently launched an energy drink of its own called KMX, which stands for nothing in particular. With Coca-Cola's sophisticated marketing department, unlimited advertising resources, and the support of some of the biggest and most successful advertising agencies in the world, will KMX overthrow Red Bull as the leading energy drink? Of course not.

If advertising was as powerful as its advocates claim, KMX ought to easily pass that Austrian upstart. But it has no chance at all, regardless of the creativity of its advertising messages or the size of its advertising budget.

Just a few years ago Coca-Cola tried the same strategy to topple Snapple, a brand that created the natural category with little advertising. Coca-Cola spent millions in the U.S. launching Fruitopia, a brand that has basically gone down the drain along with cases of Coca-Cola's money.

Do you know of any market leader that was toppled by a superior advertising campaign? Except for Altoids, we don't.

For all the accolades lavished on its advertising (Avis is only No. 2 in rent-a-cars, so why go with us? We try harder), has Avis toppled Hertz as the rent-a-car leader? Of course not.

For all the awards won by Pepsi-Cola commercials ("The Pepsi Challenge," "The Pepsi Generation"), has Pepsi toppled Coca-Cola as the cola leader? Of course not.

For all the buzz created by its Bunny advertising, has Energizer toppled Duracell as the leading appliance battery? Of course not.

Advertising agencies often believe that marketing is a battle of advertisements, rather than a battle of products. When Wells, Rich, Greene got the Royal Crown cola account a number of years ago, agency founder Mary Wells Lawrence said, "We're out to kill Coke and Pepsi. I hope you'll excuse the word, but we're really out for the jugular."

The only brand that got killed was Royal Crown. Its market share today is half of what it was when Wells, Rich, Greene got the account.

Advertising has no legitimate role to play in brand building. Advertising's role is defensive in nature. Advertising can only protect a brand once it's established.

Building Book Brands

When was the last time an advertising campaign built a book into a best-seller? Publicity certainly has. And word of mouth sometimes has. But advertising, never.

Current best-sellers such as Spencer Johnson's *Who Moved My Cheese?*, Jack Welch's *Jack: Straight from the Gut*, J. K. Rowling's Harry Potter series, and Jonathan Franzen's *The Corrections* have all received an enormous amount of publicity.

No books have ever received as much publicity as the Harry Potter series, and sales show it. The total U.S. print run of the four Harry Potter books is an astounding 65 million copies.

The publisher of the Franzen book, for example, printed an extra half million copies of *The Corrections* after the book was chosen by Oprah Winfrey for her book club. How many prime-time television commercials would it take to equal one nod from Oprah? It boggles the mind.

Every book featured on Oprah's monthly book club has made the *New York Times* best-seller list. In a recent year forty-two out of the top one hundred books were either mentioned on her show or the authors were interviewed by her. Phillip C. McGraw (Dr. Phil), Oprah's resident expert on human behavior, has had three straight *New York Times* No.1 best-selling books, including his latest, *Self Matters*.

Spencer Johnson, coauthor of *The One Minute Manager*, is a PR genius. Before his latest book, *Who Moved My Cheese?*, was published, Dr. Johnson spent several years sending galleys of his book to CEOs of Fortune 500 companies and other influential people.

Big companies were quick to respond to this personal touch. The Bank of Hawaii ordered 4,000 copies for its staff. Mercedes-Benz, 7,000 copies. Southwest Airlines, 27,000 copies. It's a classic example of the slow-buildup technique, critical in a PR program today.

"It was a very slow building, grassroots phenomenon, driven completely by word of mouth with absolutely no traditional advertising or marketing," says Dr. Johnson.

When Tony Soprano told his psychiatrist, on the HBO series *The Sopranos*, that he liked Sun Tzu's *The Art of War*, the book jumped to No. 6 on *USA Today*'s best-seller list. The publisher had to print another 25,000 copies of the twenty-four-hundred-year-old book.

Building Drug Brands

Look how Cipro became a household word because of the publicity surrounding the anthrax attacks. And Viagra became the fastest-selling new drug in history, not because of advertising, but because of publicity. The painkillers Vioxx, Vicodin, and OxyContin also received massive amounts of publicity.

Viagra, the first drug for erectile dysfunction, or impotence. Prozac, the first drug for depression. Valium, the first drug for anxiety. These and many other drug brands became famous by doing two things exceptionally well: (1) being first in a new category; (2) using publicity extensively.

PR for prescription drugs usually involves publicity at an early stage, sometimes years before the product is launched. Pleconaril, the first drug for the common cold, recently received an immense amount of publicity. So did Xolair, the first prescription drug to block IgE, the chemical that triggers allergic reactions in asthma attacks.

After a prescription drug has become successful with PR techniques, it can shift to advertising to maintain its success. The five most heavily advertised drugs (Vioxx, Prilosec, Claritin, Paxil, and Zocor) are already among the ten largest-selling drugs. The role of prescription drug advertising is not to make a drug a best-seller, but to keep a drug a best-seller.

PR can also be used to rebuild a drug brand that newer brands have passed by. Look at the success of Bayer aspirin, which has had a recent resurgence thanks to publicity about the use of aspirin in saving lives when taken during a suspected heart attack. Aspirin also benefits from its reputation as a drug to prevent future heart attacks and strokes.

Building Toy Brands

Without publicity, it's hard to create a successful toy brand today. With publicity, the sky's the limit. Cabbage Patch Kids, Furby, Teletubbies, Ninja Turtles, Mighty Morphin' Power Rangers, Beanie Babies, Barney, Pokémon—all floated to the top on a wave of publicity. And look at the continuing publicity for Barbie dolls, Monopoly games, and LEGO sets.

In 1996, Rosie O'Donnell almost single-handedly created a national obsession for Tickle Me Elmo by promoting the toy (unsolicited and uncompensated) on her television talk show.

When you study the track record of a PR program, you can usually find a Rosie moment. The single event that causes a cascade of publicity. You can't plan these magic moments, but you need to be prepared for them when they happen.

You also need to be prepared if your publicity becomes too successful.

It's the difference between a fad and a trend. Brands that take off too quickly are likely to sputter out just as quickly. They are fads. They are here today, gone tomorrow.

Trends are different. They are slow to live and slow to die. They have never had an explosion of popularity typical of a fad.

The last thing you want to do is to turn your brand into a fad. "Nobody goes there anymore," said Yogi Berra, "it was getting too popular."

What happens to fads? They go as quickly as they come. In 1983, Coleco Industries introduced Cabbage Patch Kids with a big PR program and no advertising. By the holiday season shoppers were fighting in the stores to buy the dolls.

Coleco's response was "more." More production, more varieties, more distribution points, more publicity. As a result, sales soared to more than $600 million worth of the dolls just two years later.

The next year Cabbage Patch sales plunged to $250 million. In 1988, Coleco Industries filed for Chapter 11 bankruptcy.

What went wrong? Coleco violated the law of fad control. You feed a fever, but you starve a fad.

ABC made the same mistake with their hot television show *Who Wants to Be a Millionaire*. Less than two years after it swept the top three places in the Nielsen ratings, talk has it that the show might be taken off the air. On average, ABC broadcast the Regis Philbin show four times a week. That's a sure way to kill a prime-time show no matter how popular it is. Once a week with a summer hiatus is plenty.

Advertising people are constantly fighting for more advertising because they want to elevate their messages "above the noise level." In advertising there's probably no such thing as too much advertising. But PR is different.

Too much PR can be as bad as too little PR. Why do you suppose toy icons like Barbie and Mickey Mouse are destined to be with us forever while Cabbage Patch Kids and Beanie Babies have had their day in the sun and are doomed to disappear and die?

At the first sign of a potential fad, you put on the brakes. Reduce production, reduce distribution points, and be unavailable to the media. You want to stretch out the adoption rate and turn the fad into a trend. But greed often gets in the way.

Take Your Time

Most PR programs, of course, never come close to creating a fad. You're lucky to create a minitrend. Sometimes it takes a while to get your PR material into the hands of the right person. When we were trying to put the concept of "positioning" into the minds of the marketing community, we started with an article in *Industrial Marketing* magazine, followed with another article in the same publication more than two years later. (*Industrial Marketing* is now *BtoB* magazine.)

One thing leads to another. The two articles lead to a number of speaking engagements, but these still weren't enough to make the idea take off. But one speech (at the Sales Executives Club of New York) led to an invitation by Rance Crain to write a series of positioning articles for *Advertising Age*.

That was the magic moment. It was this series entitled "The Positioning Era Cometh" that made the concept take off.

Shortly thereafter the *Wall Street Journal* did a front-page story on the subject; then the *Los Angeles Times* and other newspapers and magazines around the world followed. Time elapsed between germination and takeoff, more than three years.

The One-Two-Three Approach

When you are trying to establish a new concept, it's sometimes helpful to use a one-two-three approach where one and two have already happened and three is the concept you are trying to promote. To establish the positioning concept, we made the following three points:

1. Back in the fifties, advertising was in the *product era*, when all you needed was a better mousetrap and some money to promote it.

2. In the sixties, advertising entered the *image era*. A company found that reputation, or image, was more important in selling a product than any specific product feature.

3. Today advertising is entering the *positioning era*. To succeed in our overcommunicated society, a company must create a position in the prospect's mind, a position that takes into consideration not only a company's strengths and weaknesses, but those of its competitors as well.

(Thanks to the publicity, we were successful in establishing the "positioning" position for our advertising agency, but we made a serious error in not taking the next step. We should have capitalized on our PR coup and dropped our advertising business and focused on strategy, which is the heart of what positioning is all about. Eventually, however, we did take that step and have been very pleased with the results.)

The successful launch of Advil in 1984 used the same one-two-three approach. The Advil message showed pictures of the three major pain relievers and then labeled each with its date of introduction: aspirin, 1899; Tylenol, 1955; Advil, 1984. Then to reinforce the idea that Advil was the newest (and presumably the best) pain reliever, the advertising used the theme "advanced medicine for pain."

The telecom industry, especially in Europe, has fallen for a similar "generational" approach to mobile phones. 1G was analog, 2G is digital, and 3G is going to be Internet-access phones. We don't think that 3G phones are going to become a big business, but the psychological appeal of this third-generation concept is very powerful.

A Blind Leap of Faith

Creating a new category often requires a blind leap of faith. You have to believe that thousands of unexplored categories are just waiting to be discovered. Unfortunately many management people have given up looking for new categories.

Instead they look to combine existing categories into combination products. Television with computers. Telephones with the Internet. The Internet with television. Cell phones with handheld computers. Computer printers with copiers, scanners, and fax machines.

Called convergence, this combination concept has received almost universal endorsement by the media. If everyone buys into the convergence concept, then the opportunity to create new brands by creating new categories will come to a screeching halt. (Those 3G phones are a convergence product, which is why we don't believe they will ever achieve much success).

As one of the strongest proponents of the new-category/new-brand approach, we have a vested interest in establishing the opposite concept, which we call divergence.

Fortunately, history is on our side. The mainframe computer, the new category that built the IBM brand, didn't converge. It diverged, creating opportunities for many new categories and brands: minicomputers (DEC), workstations (Sun Microsystems), computer storage (EMC), personal computers (Compaq), direct sales of personal computers (Dell), personal computer software (Microsoft).

Television, the new category that built the ABC, CBS, and NBC brands, didn't converge. It diverged, creating opportunities for many new categories and brands: cable television (ESPN, CNN), premium cable television (HBO, Showtime), satellite television (DirecTV, EchoStar).

Up till now, unfortunately, we have been unable to get the media on our side. For eight years we have been trying to place an article on divergence, with little success. So we keep trying different approaches, and sooner or later we are going to succeed.

The longer the gestation process, the bigger the story. An elephant takes two years to be born.

The Whitestrips Story

Procter & Gamble is spending $90 million in a classic marketing program to launch Crest Whitestrips, $40 million of which is being spent on traditional TV and print advertising. (The product is a box of clear plastic strips that consumers wear over their teeth in half-hour intervals twice a day to whiten their teeth.)

But this is the PR era, and in our opinion, P&G is making three basic mistakes.

1. *Launching the Whitestrips program with an advertising rather than a PR campaign.* Sure PR is undoubtedly playing a role in the Whitestrips campaign, but you take the wind out of PR's sails when you start the program with advertising. Media usually won't run stories about products they see advertised.

   PR needs several years to establish a new category like Whitestrips, let alone the brand name. As it happens, there's a good publicity story in the product. It's the only one of its kind on the market, and P&G has a dozen patents on the product.

   Instead of credentials, the Whitestrips TV commercials were loaded with creativity. The agency supervisor explained the idea behind the campaign: "Things you wouldn't expect to be white become white just by touching the package." The commercials show ants and a chameleon turning white by crawling over a Whitestrips package. Creative, yes. Believable, no. (The animals didn't last long. Whitestrips has gone back to more traditional advertising.)

2. *Using a line extension name.* Crest is a toothpaste brand. Putting the Crest name on the new Whitestrips product helps neither Whitestrips nor the toothpaste.

A revolutionary development like white teeth needs a new brand name. (Levi Strauss first launched its line of casual slacks with the name Levi's Tailored Classics before they got smart and changed the name to Dockers.)

It's easier to remember one name than it is two or three. If a consumer wants to buy a pair of casual slacks, he just has to remember Dockers rather than Levi's Tailored Classics. If you want to buy the new Procter & Gamble product, you have to remember two names, Crest Whitestrips. A new brand name would have reduced that to one.

What's a Crest? Crest was the first decay-prevention toothpaste and the first toothpaste to receive the American Dental Association's seal of approval. The torrent of favorable publicity helped build the brand.

Over time, brands decay. Crest needs to maintain its toothpaste brand with advertising. For the most part, however, Crest has used its advertising to launch new flavors, new packaging, and new line extensions. This is one of the reasons it recently lost its toothpaste leadership position to Colgate.

Crest Whitestrips is not going to get Crest toothpaste its leadership position back.

3. *Failing to give the new product a meaningful category name.* Whitestrips, of course, is a registered trademark of Procter & Gamble. To get around trademark regulations, underneath the Whitestrips name (in small type) are the words *dental whitening system.*

Are consumers going to use the words *dental whitening systems?* No, they're not. They're going to refer to the category as, "whitestrips." Furthermore, as soon as competitors figure out how to get around P&G's patents, they will introduce whitening strips, clear strips, dental strips, bright strips, smile strips, etc.

In fact, competitive dental whitening systems (but not the Whitestrips-type product) are already on the market with names like Dazzling White, Natural White, Dental White, Rapid White, Finally White, Sonic White, and Plus White.

Then there are toothpaste whitening products that also confuse the issue: Ultra Brite Advanced Whitening, Colgate Platinum Whitening, and Crest Extra Whitening.

Sooner or later Procter & Gamble's dental-whitening-system brand will become Crest and not Whitestrips. (Miller Lite fell into the same line-extension trap as Crest Whitestrips. Over time *Lite* became nothing but a generic word denoting the light beer category, and the brand's identity became Miller, thereby causing confusion with all the other Miller brands. The same thing will happen with Crest Whitestrips.)

Line extensions cause two problems: (1) they blur the singular identity of the brand; (2) they bleed advertising support from the base brand.

A Brand with No PR Potential?

What if a proposed new product or service has no publicity potential? Many marketers jump off the PR bandwagon as soon as they find themselves saddled with a brand that is shunned by the press.

We have no choice, is the excuse, so we have to use advertising to launch our new brand. This is the most important issue in marketing today: how to launch a brand with no, or limited, publicity potential.

This was the issue facing Coca-Cola as they prepared to launch the KMX brand to compete with Red Bull. Sure, Coca-Cola received some KMX publicity, but it wasn't very favorable. In truth, the KMX publicity probably helped Red Bull more than it did Coca-Cola. If Coca-Cola was launching an energy drink, the category had to be getting important and the company had to be worried about the success of Red Bull was the media's interpretation of the KMX launch.

If there's ever a case against building brands with advertising, it's the experience of Coca-Cola. Here is a company that owns the world's most valuable brand, a company that does $20 billion in annual sales, a company that has the most powerful distribution network in the soft drink industry, and a company that employs some of the world's most prestigious advertising agencies. Yet KMX is certain to become another Coca-Cola marketing disappointment.

In soft drink niche markets, being second is being nowhere. Unless you are first in a new category, it's difficult to get the media's attention.

After the success of Dr Pepper, Coca-Cola tried Mr. Pibb, with little success.

After the success of PepsiCo's Mountain Dew, Coca-Cola tried Mello Yellow, with little success. Recently Coca-Cola tried Surge, which didn't work either.

After the success of Starbucks' Frappuccino, Coca-Cola tried Planet Java. The outcome is still in doubt, but does anyone think that Planet Java has a chance to become a big brand like Frappuccino? We don't.

How do you launch a brand with no publicity potential?

The sad truth is, you don't. In this media-saturated environment, you win or lose in the press. If you can't win the media battle, you can't win the marketing battle.

The media is the battleground. A marketing manager who launches a brand with no hope of winning the PR war is in the same position as a military general who launches a frontal attack against an entrenched enemy.

Yet the Charge of the Light Brigade happens every day in the marketing arena. Companies launch brands, often line extensions, with massive advertising programs and no publicity potential. This is a deadly combination. It assures high monetary losses coupled with little hope of marketing success.

But PR is not just for new brands. Old brands often need PR, too.

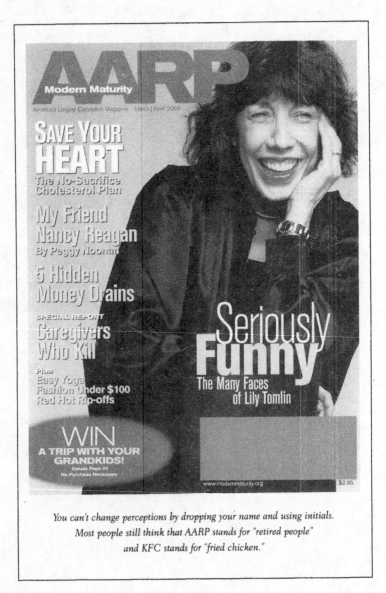

You can't change perceptions by dropping your name and using initials.
Most people still think that AARP stands for "retired people"
and KFC stands for "fried chicken."

12

Rebuilding *an* Old Brand *with* PR

When we write about "building a brand," we're not just writing about new brands. We're writing about all brands that are nowhere in the mind. A fifty-year-old brand that is nowhere in the mind is no different from a brand-new brand . . . from a strategy point of view. Both have to start with PR to establish their credentials before they can switch to advertising.

Truth to say, most brands are nowhere in the mind. It's only a relatively few brands that have established enough credentials to be able to profitably employ an advertising strategy.

Even a well-known brand with an established position will need PR first if it plans to change its position. Just because your name is well known doesn't mean you can change your position at the drop of an advertising hat. Life doesn't work that way. Perceptions are difficult to change, especially when you try to change them with advertising.

Rebuilding the AARP Brand

What do you think about an organization called AARP? What does AARP stand for? Most people would say "retired people," as in the American Association of Retired People.

Most people are wrong. Many AARP members are still working, so in 1998 the American Association of Retired People changed its name to AARP.

The new name was a nonstory because it didn't do anything to change what AARP stood for in the mind. You can't walk away from your past by changing your name to initials. Was Kentucky Fried Chicken able to walk away from "fried" by changing its name to KFC? Was the International House of Pancakes able to walk away from "pancakes" by changing its name to IHOP? In many ways, it's the opposite. The Home of the Whopper often calls itself B.K. because it's an involving way of saying Burger King.

Since AARP was trying to change how it was perceived, the organization should have started with a clean sheet of paper and developed a program with some publicity potential. (No publicity, no change of perception. It's as simple as that.)

There are a number of interesting social changes that AARP could have developed a PR program around.

There's no story in the fact that AARP doesn't want to be associated with the word *retired*. The only story is in what AARP wants to be known for. And what is that? Our suggestion: replace *retired* with *revitalizing*, as in the American Association for Revitalizing People.

Put the emphasis on education for the changes that are going to take place in your life after your first 50 years. (Our suggested theme: help for the second half of your life.)

Goals change. At age twenty-one, a person might want a job with a future, a job that provides prestige and plenty of money. At age fifty, the eligibility age for becoming an AARP member, a person might want a job with a purpose where he or she could make a difference and find fulfillment.

People are living longer. At age twenty-one, a person can expect to work for twenty-nine years before becoming AARP material. Yet at age fifty, a person can expect to live another thirty-four years. If you can manage to live to be fifty, you still have, on average, more than half your adult life ahead of you.

People are also working longer. A recent survey shows that 40 percent plan to keep working for pay after retirement. An equal number plan on doing volunteer work. (Think Jimmy Carter.)

We also suggested a new name for AARP's magazine, *Modern Maturity*. (Who wants to be mature?) Our suggestion: *Act II*.

Interestingly enough, AARP recently launched a Spanish-language version of *Modern Maturity* with an excellent name, *Segunda Juventud*, or "second youth" in English.

(Now that the new head of the AARP is a former high-ranking PR person, perhaps the association will be taking some steps in this direction in the future.)

The solution to a PR problem is invariably a single, simple focus. But it takes courage to decide what single aspect of a situation to focus on. The American Cancer Society promotes awareness of the seven danger signals of cancer, but how many people can name even one?

Rebuilding the Heart Brand

The American Heart Association is in the same situation as AARP and the American Cancer Society. Everybody knows the association, but nobody knows what it stands for.

Currently the American Heart Association is promoting awareness of (a) the three warning signs of a heart attack, (b) the five warning signs of a stroke, and (c) the five rules for a healthier heart. In addition the association promotes awareness of (d) the five less common warning signs of a heart attack in women.

Name one.

What is the heart? In mythology, the heart is the center of love and romance. In reality, the heart is a pump. Mechanisms of all types need pumps. Automobiles, washing machines, human beings. Big cars and big washing machines have big pumps. Small cars and small washing machines have small pumps.

One of the biggest health problems in America today is obesity. According to the surgeon general, 61 percent of adults are overweight; 27 percent are obese. People who put on the pounds can't go to a garage for a larger pump. (More than 300,000 deaths each year are connected with weight-related illnesses.)

One of the rules for a healthier heart is "maintaining proper weight." This is the single idea that we believe the American Heart Association should focus on. As it happens, no other major health association focuses on the obesity problem.

Rebuilding the Bacardi Brand

Bacardi is a brand that doesn't need rebuilding. It's already the largest-selling distilled spirit in America and has been for the last twenty years. (Not just the largest-selling rum, but the largest-selling distilled spirit.)

The question is, could Bacardi be more successful than it already is? We think so.

The classic rum drink is rum and Coke, which still accounts for about half of rum's consumption in the United States. But as you might expect, Bacardi has spent most of its marketing dollars trying to broaden the brand. Rum martinis, rum and tonic, rum and orange juice, rum piña coladas, rum daiquiris.

What PR strategy would you use to promote Bacardi rum?

We suggested that Bacardi narrow its focus. Go back to the drink that made them famous. Go back to promoting rum and Coke.

Serendipity is a useful attribute for a PR person. As it happens, Cuba Libre is the name for the drink made with rum and Coca-Cola and lime juice. In fact, Bacardi claims the first Cuba Libre was made with its product in the year 1898.

"Cuba Libre" is also an ideal rallying cry for a liquor company that was kicked out of Cuba in 1959 when Castro's communists took over. No company has a more vested interest in a free Cuba than Bacardi Limited, which was forced to relocate to Puerto Rico.

There are hundreds of ways to use "Cuba Libre" in a publicity campaign. One thought is to call a Cuba Libre "the only mixed drink that demonstrates both your good taste and your politics." And think of the party Bacardi could throw when Fidel finally meets his maker.

Rebuilding the MARTA Brand

Sometimes the PR strategist will need to add a totally new idea to the brand. We live in Atlanta, a city that has a lot going for it including hills, trees, growing businesses, and a great airport. One thing that is not going too well in Atlanta is the traffic.

To solve the traffic problem, we have MARTA (Metropolitan Atlanta Rapid Transit Authority). What PR strategy would you use to get people out of their cars and into a bus or train?

Many social problems are similar to the Atlanta commuting problem. The drug problem, the alcohol problem, the obesity problem. People know all the reasons they shouldn't take drugs or drink too much or eat too much, but they do it anyway.

People know all of the reasons why they shouldn't drive their cars to work, but they do it anyway. Conventional advertising programs are a waste of money, and PR programs based on conventional advertising themes are just as useless.

After thinking about the problem, here is what we would do. First of all, divorce the buses from the trains. Even better, give the buses a different name and reserve the MARTA name for the trains.

A bus isn't exactly a "rapid transit" vehicle. Furthermore the car owner, the real prospect for the campaign, sees the bus rider as someone who can't afford an automobile. Moving from a car to a bus would be tantamount to stepping down in status, always a difficult sell.

Focus on the MARTA trains. Narrowing the focus is a good idea for any marketing program. It gives you something tangible to work with. (Many companies market a broad line of products or services to offer customers "greater choice." By doing so, however, they often undermine the publicity potential of their product line.)

How do we move Mercury, Mercedes, and Mitsubishi drivers to become MARTA riders? Specifically, how do we move them to MARTA if they already know the benefits of doing so? (Only 4 percent of all Atlanta commuters use MARTA trains. And 78 percent of car commuters travel alone.)

You let them sample the system. (You don't sell a new drink by telling people how great it's going to taste. You let them sample it.)

"MARTA Mondays" is our concept. Every Monday, everyone rides free on MARTA trains. Once a week MARTA should let prospects sample the system to see how much time it takes, how comfortable it is, how far it is to the nearest MARTA station, etc.

A high fixed-cost system, such as a rail network, is ideal for free sampling. The cost of carrying additional riders is minimal. Sure, MARTA would lose money on some regular riders, but not those who buy weekly or monthly commuter tickets. Every good idea involves some sacrifice.

What are the chances of MARTA actually adopting the MARTA Mondays idea? Not very promising. "What? Give away our service for free? Forget it."

(It is easier for a camel to go through the eye of a needle than for a breakthrough idea to enter into the kingdom of the corporation.)

Alliteration, Repetition, and Rhyme

If you want a memorable rallying cry for your brand, we strongly suggest alliteration, repetition, and rhyme. MARTA Mondays is a much more effective slogan than MARTA Tuesdays.

History shows that slogans which use one or more of these memory-enhancing techniques can be extremely long-lasting.

- Fifty-four forty or fight.
- Loose lips sink ships.
- To be or not to be.
- Shop till you drop.
- He who laughs last, laughs best.
- Toys for tots.
- Liar, liar, pants on fire.
- *Debbie Does Dallas.*

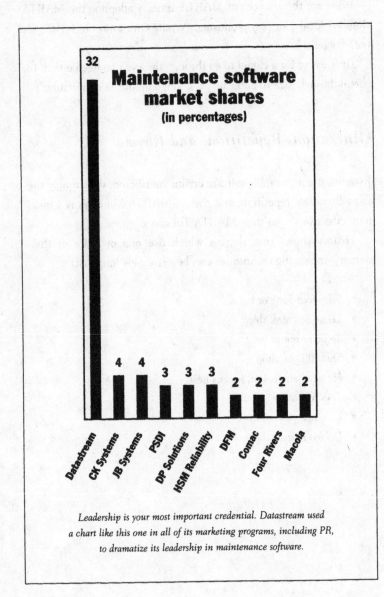

**Maintenance software
market shares**
(in percentages)

Datastream	CK Systems	JB Systems	PSDI	DP Solutions	HSM Reliability	DFM	Comac	Four Rivers	Macola
32	4	4	3	3	3	2	2	2	2

*Leadership is your most important credential. Datastream used
a chart like this one in all of its marketing programs, including PR,
to dramatize its leadership in maintenance software.*

13

Establishing Your Credentials

Even if they spell your name right, some publicity is useless.

What publicity is useful? Those stories, articles, and features that help establish your credentials.

A story on energy drinks that mentions Red Bull, but doesn't mention its leadership in the category, can actually be harmful. A story on automobile safety that doesn't mention Volvo's safety leadership can also hurt the brand.

On the other hand, a positive story that helps a brand establish leadership in its category can be worth its weight in gold.

That's why you can't measure publicity as if it were an advertising buy. What the PR industry calls "ad value equivalency" makes no sense. The objective of a PR program (building a brand) is something that, except in special circumstances, advertising cannot do. How can you equate the two? It's like valuing a B-52 bomber in terms of the number of infantry troops it's equivalent to.

Still, some companies do equate the two. There's a story making the rounds that CBS gave Dr Pepper a free Super Bowl spot that normally cost about $2 million as a damage payment for a remark made by David Letterman. (He likened the soft drink to "sewer water.")

When you want to establish a leadership claim, it's especially important to use media to give your brand the credentials it needs. It's not enough to get stories in newspapers, articles in magazines, or interviews on radio or television, although these can help.

What is absolutely necessary is to get your leadership claims authenticated by the media.

The Datastream Story

We helped a maintenance software company called Datastream get off the ground. One of our suggestions was to print a bar chart with market share data and send the chart along with all press releases.

The bar chart, we pointed out, would dramatize the extent of Datastream's leadership. The company had a larger market share than its next eleven competitors combined. Furthermore, charts like this one discourage prospects from considering any of the "also-rans." If a prospect is going to consider one of the smaller brands, he or she should probably consider them all, and that seems like just too much trouble. It's an easier decision to go with the leader, Datastream.

But didn't both prospects and the press know that Datastream was the leader? Not at all. Back in 1993, there were 150 suppliers who had sold only 27,700 maintenance software packages out of a total potential market of some 250,000 to 750,000 packages. In other words, market penetration was only 4 to 11 percent. (And this percentage was probably overestimated.)

Datastream went on to dominate the maintenance software market, a position the company occupies today.

The Starbucks Story

One of the best ways to establish your leadership credentials is by being the first brand in a new category. Starbucks was the first European-style coffee bar. Furthermore, the Starbucks stores attracted the young, urban, hip crowd. Naturally the media fawned over both the concept and the customers.

"It is now difficult to launch a product through consumer advertising because customers don't really pay attention as they did in the past, nor do they believe the message," said Howard Schultz, Starbucks' chairman and founder. "I look at the money spent on advertising, and it surprises me that people still believe they are getting returns on their investments."

We're not Starbucks, some clients have told us, we don't have cappuccino, latte, or any exciting products to talk about. That's a common problem today.

(Back in the days when automobiles had expensive modular radios, some car owners tried to stop break-ins by posting No Radio signs on the inside of their windshields. One owner returned to find someone had broken his window and scribbled "Get one" on the sign.)

No exciting product to talk about? Get one. This is the job of the PR strategist today. Find an idea that will generate publicity. And not any kind of publicity either. Publicity that will build a brand.

Establishing a New Category

The new category doesn't have to be earth-shattering either. PowerBar was the first energy bar. Heineken was the first high-priced imported beer. Razor was the first high-tech scooter.

When your brand represents a new category that captures the

attention of the media, the publicity fallout can be incredible. When Polaroid introduced instant photography, Dr. Land and his new camera made the cover of *Time* magazine, the news shows on network television, and virtually every other important publicity medium. Literally, the publicity made the Polaroid brand.

When Xerox introduced the plain-paper copier, the same thing happened. The publicity built the brand, not the advertising.

The proper role and function of advertising is after the fact. After the brand has been established, after the brand has credibility in the prospect's mind, you can use advertising to reinforce and remind prospects. Advertising is the infantry that follows up a tank or an air attack. You would never launch a military attack with infantry alone. Why would you launch a marketing attack with advertising alone?

The Miraclesuit Story

Sometimes there is no inherent PR idea in the brand. It's just another product or service. With the advertising crowd, this is not a problem. If the product is not exciting, then what the client needs is exciting advertising, i.e., creativity. (We believe we have already demonstrated the futility of the creative approach in advertising.)

The PR crowd, however, has to add something to the brand to generate publicity. Public relations is the discipline that requires the creativity.

Sometimes you can do it with words alone. In 1992, A&H Sportswear introduced a women's swimsuit whose weft-lock construction provided optimal stretch and control in both directions of the fabric (other swimwear stretches in only one direction). They even gave their new product an exciting name, Miraclesuit. But it was the PR agency Burson-Marsteller that verbalized the benefits of the brand: "Look ten pounds lighter in ten seconds." (The ten seconds it takes to put it on.)

With publicity only, no advertising, Miraclesuit became a successful brand. Even though the suit sells in the designer sections of department stores at a 20 to 25 percent higher price than the average swimsuit, Miraclesuit has become the number two brand in the market, second only to Nautica.

Ten years later, now that the brand is established, and the publicity potential has run its course, it may be time to switch Micraclesuit from a PR horse to an advertising horse. And what should Miraclesuit's advertising strategy be? "Look ten pounds lighter in ten seconds."

What do you suppose the odds are that a future Miraclesuit advertising agency would actually use such a strategy? Slim to none at all. The advertising business is focused on creativity, the search for the new and different. From our personal experience, we know it's difficult for a new advertising agency to adopt an idea created by a previous agency. It's going to be even more difficult for an advertising agency to adopt a strategy developed by a PR agency. It's the NCH factor, "not created here."

(There is a role and function for advertising, but it's not based on creativity. It's based on plagiarism. The ad agency of the future will need to build "follow-up" campaigns using ideas and images already planted in the prospect's mind by PR campaigns.)

NEW YORK TIMES BESTSELLER

ANITA DIAMANT

THE

RED

TENT

A NOVEL

*A typical PR program starts slowly, often with a
single brilliant idea. The Red Tent, a novel
by Anita Diamant, was going nowhere until
the publisher sent copies to rabbis.*

14

Rolling Out
Your Brand

After lukewarm sales, *The Red Tent*, a first novel by an unknown author (Anita Diamant), was scheduled for pulping. When Ms. Diamant was offered the leftover stock at a dollar apiece, she suggested instead that the publisher send copies to rabbis. (The book was a fictionalized life of Dinah, only sister of Joseph, owner of the coat of many colors.)

It worked. Two and a half years after its publication, *The Red Tent* became a best-seller. The paperback edition has sold some 2 million copies and Hollywood has optioned the book.

To Dance with the White Dog, a novel by author Terry Kay, sat dormant in Japan for six years. Then a submanager of a small city bookstore in Japan liked the book so much he wrote an in-store review telling customers how great the book was.

As a result, the store sold 471 copies in one month, an amazing figure for a small bookstore. Then a twenty-three-year-old salesperson for the book's Japanese publisher persuaded her boss to distribute the handwritten review nationwide. Newspapers and TV stations picked up the story, and now half a million copies are in print in Japan, twice as many copies as have been sold in the United States since *White Dog* was first published in 1990.

A tiny spark sets in motion a publicity program that sells half a million books? Sure, it happens all the time. Unfortunately, when the brand gets to be big and famous, when the brand gets to the top of the mountain, management tends to erase the tracks that took it there. They pretend that it was born at the top or at least got there by its own merits. Certainly it didn't get there via favorable publicity.

The Keystone Placement

In PR today, one of the most effective tactics is to place a "keystone" story. This is a positive story in a key publication (or television show) that can support the entire publicity program.

On April 28, 1997, the front page of the "Marketplace" section of the *Wall Street Journal* carried a major story about Papa John's pizza ("Popular Pizza Chain's Gimmick Is Taste").

Papa John's theme was "better ingredients, better pizza."

Instead of sauce made from concentrate, Papa John's uses sauce made from vine-ripened, fresh-packed tomatoes. Instead of various cheeses, Papa John's uses 100 percent mozzarella cheese. Instead of frozen dough, Papa John's uses fresh dough. Instead of tap water for the dough, Papa John's uses purified water.

As the months roll on, a keystone story is likely to be sliced and diced into many other stories. No reporter is going to do a story about Papa John's without first checking what the *Wall Street Journal* had to say about the company, and thanks to the Internet this is easy to do.

It's easy to miss the essence of Papa John's success. It wasn't just an unveiling of product benefits (we have this benefit and they don't). The essence of the story was that Papa John's was the first premium or upscale pizza. The benefits support the premium position. This element of "firstness" enabled Papa John's to win the publicity war. *You can't get famous if you're not first in something.*

Rolling Out a Doughnut Brand

Sometimes it takes a while for a new company to find something to be first in. Industrial Luncheon Services was founded in 1946 as a catering business. Two years later the company had some two hundred canteen trucks, twenty-five factory cafeterias, and a vending unit. When founder William Rosenberg looked at his sales figures, he noticed that 40 percent of his truck sales were coffee and doughnuts. This observation turned a modestly successful regional caterer into a worldwide brand.

Rosenberg narrowed his focus by opening a coffee-and-doughnut shop that eventually became Dunkin' Donuts, the first doughnut shop with a counter where customers could eat on the premises.

Today, Dunkin' Donuts is the largest coffee-and-doughnut chain in the world, with nearly 5,000 sites in the United States and thirty-five other countries. (The rest of Rosenberg's catering business is long since gone.)

Then there's Krispy Kreme, today's "hot" doughnut. Krispy Kreme focused on the depth of doughnut depravity, the glazed doughnut, and made it to the top on a whirlwind of publicity.

Shortly before a Krispy Kreme shop opened in a suburb of Phoenix, Sheriff Joe Arpaio, who bills himself as "the toughest sheriff in America," asked whether he could be the first customer. Krispy Kreme gladly obliged Mr. Arpaio, who has become a local celebrity by requiring his prisoners to wear pink underwear.

The sheriff ate his doughnut before the TV cameras and then uttered the perfect sound bite: "These doughnuts are so good they should be illegal."

What ignited another firestorm of Krispy Kreme publicity was its April 2000 IPO. Going public never tasted so good. It's usually a good PR move for a brand on the rise to plan an initial public offering.

When You Don't Need to Be First

Life is unfair. You can't get famous if you're not first in something. But if you are already famous, your product doesn't need to be a "first" to produce a boatload of publicity. Look at the massive publicity generated by Microsoft's Xbox video-game console and Microsoft's Windows operating system.

Edelman PR, for example, generated hundreds of major news stories for the Xbox before the advertising began to run. The launch was so successful that within two weeks the Xbox was the largest-selling video-game console.

Why can't we get publicity like Microsoft? some clients have asked us. You're not Microsoft, is our reply. Publicity is like money. The poor need it and the rich don't. So who gets all the money? The rich. So who gets all the publicity? The companies that don't need it.

You see this inequality in newspaper headlines. "Microsoft Explores a New Territory: Fun" was the headline of a story about the Xbox in the *New York Times*. But the *Wall Street Journal*'s story didn't say "Papa John's Gimmick Is Taste," it said "Popular Pizza Chain's Gimmick Is Taste." (Papa John's wasn't famous enough to make it into the headline.)

Up and Down the Mountain

PR is essentially a two-step game: (1) up the mountain, and (2) down the mountain.

When you're building a brand, you are pushing it up the media mountain. You don't start at the top, nor is the ascent easy.

When you get to the top, when you have a mighty brand like

Microsoft, your strategy should change, too. You become selective. You don't place phone calls, you take them. You turn down many more media requests than you accept. Your strategy is not to publicize the brand but to protect the brand from negative publicity.

On the way up, your strategy is to "roll out the brand." Take whatever the media will give you, which is usually not a story on network TV or in one of the Big Five newspapers. More often than not, you have to start small in some obscure publication and then "roll out" the story into more important media.

Every brand that gets to the top got there by favorable publicity. It may have been a better product, but without publicity it's not going to go anywhere. When you are pushing your brand up media mountain, a celebrity CEO can be enormously helpful. Where would Ben & Jerry's, the first socially responsible ice cream, be without Ben Cohen and Jerry Greenfield? The two hippie entrepreneurs made Ben & Jerry's the brand it is today.

Unlike PR programs, which usually start small, advertising programs are inevitably based on the big-bang concept. "Let's launch this program with the most intensive advertising barrage ever created by any company anywhere in the world" seems to be the watchword.

You can't use the same big-bang strategy with a public relations program. Every brand needs its own timetable. Normally you need publicity in some small medium before you can move on (or roll out) the program to the next, more important medium.

You have to give your PR efforts enough time to produce results. Impatience kills more good PR ideas than poor execution. The better the idea, the longer it is going to take to implant that idea into someone's mind. It's new, it's different, and it's instantly under suspicion. Media people are sometimes just as skeptical as consumers.

Building the "Positioning" Brand

The "positioning" idea that Jack Trout and I pioneered went from a small trade publication (*Industrial Marketing*) to a larger, more important trade publication (*Advertising Age*), and then to the *Wall Street Journal*.

Notice that the *Wall Street Journal* picked up the story from a trade publication, but would not have run the story if it had appeared in the *New York Times, Time, Newsweek,* or any major consumer publication.

You violate the publicity "pecking order" at your own peril. The *Wall Street Journal*, for example, won't do a story that has already appeared in *USA Today*. On the other hand, *USA Today* might do its own version of a story that first appeared in the *Wall Street Journal.*

The television networks don't care where a story has already appeared. They only care about the quality of the spokesperson and whether or not the public is interested in the story. That's why a barrage of publicity in the print media is the ideal launching ground for a television appearance.

Every major TV appearance that we have made (*CBS Early Show, NBC Nightly News, ABC World News Tonight,* CNN, CNBC, etc.) was sparked by a print story in some medium.

No one reads the media more than the media. How come we didn't have this story? is a typical question an editor might ask. "Find a new angle and let's do our own story next week."

It's these relationships that are at the core of the rollout strategy. You need to carefully consider which publications want new ideas and which publications will run stories only after they have gained credibility in other media.

Naturally, there are always exceptions to every rule. If you have a branding story that is so powerful that it can create media hype almost all by itself, then you can release the story simultaneously to all media. The launch of Viagra, the first prescription drug for erectile dysfunction, was that type of story. In the history of marketing, however, there are not many brands that have risen as fast as Viagra.

Building the Mustang Brand

No industry depends on advertising as much as the automotive industry. Last year, seven of the thirteen largest advertising budgets were for automobile brands (Chevrolet, Dodge, Toyota, Ford, Nissan, Chrysler, and Honda). Together these brands spent $4 billion on advertising, enough money to fight a small war.

These seven brands sold 11,108,832 cars last year, and for each car sold these seven brands spent $359.12 on advertising.

Do you remember any single automobile advertisement or commercial? And especially, do you remember any commercial that changed your mind about which automobile brand you wanted to buy? Most people can't.

In spite of these massive expenditures, advertising plays a minor role in selling cars. Buyers are much more influenced by street visibility, word of mouth by owners, editorial coverage in automotive sections of daily newspapers, etc.

You have to go all the way back to 1964 to find an automobile brand introduced the right way, the Ford Mustang. News about the Mustang, the first sports car for people who don't like to drive sports cars, was leaked to the media for almost a year before its formal introduction (the slow buildup).

Six months before the launch, Lee Iacocca invited key journalists to preview the car. Press kits were mailed to thousands of newspapers and magazines. Two hundred disc jockeys were flown in to test-drive the cars and then were lent white Mustangs for a week.

Finally, on April 13, 1964, the car's public introduction took place in conjunction with the opening of Ford's pavilion at the New York World's Fair. Following the World's Fair bash, the assembled journalists drove a group of early production cars from New York to Detroit.

The resultant publicity was incredible. Iacocca and his Mustang appeared on the covers of *Time* and *Newsweek* the same week, the first time that had ever happened.

Sales were incredible, too. It took only four months to sell the first 100,000 Mustangs. More than 400,000 were sold in the first year. Two years into production, the millionth Mustang rolled off the production line accompanied by the usual publicity barrage.

A new category, a celebrity spokesperson, a slow buildup, and a launch date tied into the opening of an international event: these were the elements of the Mustang's publicity success. The stars won't always line up like this for your brand, but it helps to plan this way.

Did Ford also spend a bundle on Mustang advertising? Sure. Did they need to? Probably not.

Advertising is often in the same category as the potion an old wrangler was throwing along the trail as he led a group through the Grand Canyon.

"What are you doing?" asked one of the group.

"I'm warding off the elephants," the wrangler replied.

"There are no elephants within five thousand miles of here."

"Effective, isn't it."

We're sure the advertising wranglers at the time were quick to claim credit for the Mustang's success. When sales are up, advertising takes a bow. When sales are down, the product gets the blame.

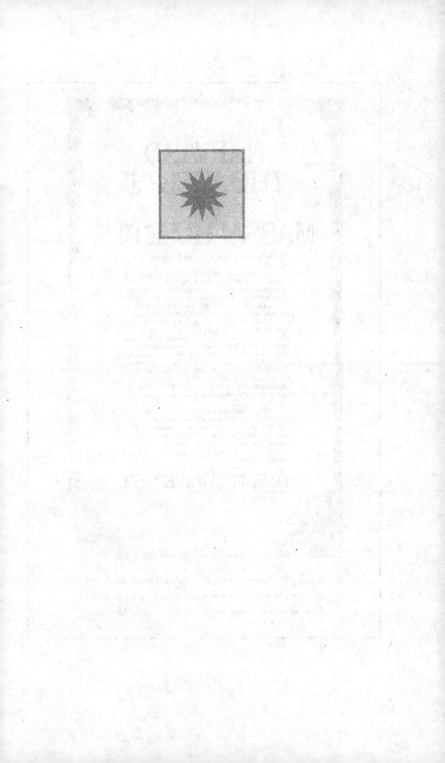

Nothing illustrates the point that you can't build brands with advertising as well as the experience at Adelphi, which tried to use advertising to put itself in the same class as Harvard.

15

Building *an* Educational Brand

While the folks at Harvard, Princeton, and Yale might not accept the term, these educational institutions have become brands. And how did they become brands? Certainly not by advertising. They became powerful brands by massive publicity even if the publicity efforts were not self-directed.

A handful of universities have tried to build brands using advertising, most notably Long Island's Adelphi University. The Adelphi campaign consisted of full-page newspapers ads with headlines like these:

- "Harvard. The Adelphi of Massachusetts."
- "Does anybody need an education this good?"
- "There are three things everyone should read before entering college: Plato's *Republic*, the complete works of Aristotle, and this ad."

What happened? Did Adelphi become the Harvard of Long Island? Silly question. What actually happened was that the president of Adelphi University got fired. You can't build a brand with advertising, which has as much credibility as a message inside a fortune cookie.

Fortune magazine is another matter. If *Fortune* had run an article calling Adelphi "the Harvard of Long Island," it would have had a serious impact on the university's fortunes. Sometimes all you need is one favorable piece from one publication or television show that you can use endlessly in article reprints, direct mail, and in PR efforts with other media. (The keystone placement.)

What Surveys Have Done for Quinnipiac

Take Quinnipiac University, for example. This small private school in Hamden, Connecticut, has a difficult name, to say the least. Over the last decade, however, the school has increased its enrollment from 1,900 to 6,000 students and nearly quintupled its budget to $115 million.

Question: How did Quinnipiac do so well when college enrollments have been sagging? Answer: the Quinnipiac Poll.

When John Lahey took over as president in 1987, he decided that good old Quinnipiac needed some publicity. So he launched the Quinnipiac Poll, with surveys on regional and national elections and other hot issues, then bombarded the media with the results. In ten years Quinnipiac has turned up in some twenty-five hundred news stories.

In the year 2000 the university spent $430,000 for forty-four surveys, fifteen of them on the Hillary Clinton Senate race.

Where one survey would probably have been a waste of money, forty-four surveys are a good use of a university's resources. The polls have put Quinnipiac on the radar screen of millions of potential students, parents, and guidance counselors.

It's not only the volume of surveys that are working for Quinnipiac, it's also the consistency of doing them year after year. That's what has put the Quinnipiac Poll in the mind of the marketplace. (Now if they would only do something about that name.)

Narrowing the Focus to Become a Leader

Note, too, how certain institutions of higher learning have built brands by following (consciously or not) the key principle of PR branding: set up a new category you can be first in. The Harvard Graduate School of Business Administration is known for "management."

You compete with Harvard not by being the same as Harvard, you compete with Harvard by being different. Wharton, the business graduate school of the University of Pennsylvania, is not the Harvard of Pennsylvania. Wharton is the leader in "finance," the first graduate school to preempt the finance category.

Kellogg, the business graduate school of Northwestern University, is not the Harvard of Illinois. Kellogg is the leader in "marketing," the first graduate school to preempt the marketing category.

As it happens, both Wharton and Kellogg don't specialize in their specialties. Both offer a full range of business school courses, but they both are better off because they created the perception of being leaders in narrow categories.

Thunderbird (official name: American Graduate School of International Management) is not the Harvard of Arizona. Thunderbird is the leader in "international studies," the first graduate school to preempt the international studies category.

What Communications Could Do for Pace

We once met with the people at Pace University, a private school in Manhattan with some 10,000 students. What is Manhattan known for? Three things: finance, fashion, and communications. Finance is Wharton. Fashion is the Fashion Institute of Technology (also located in Manhattan). That leaves communications.

Pace University should be a "communications" school. Manhattan is the communications center of the world. ABC, CBS, NBC, the *New York Times*, the *Wall Street Journal, Time, Newsweek,* and virtually the entire magazine industry are located in Manhattan. What better location for a communications school?

We can't do that, said Pace officials. Students want a full range of courses. According to the university: "For nearly a century, the mission of Pace University has been creating opportunity through preparation and education for the sons and daughters of New York."

Maybe so, but most sons and daughters of New York also want to go to a university that's famous in the hopes that some of that fame might rub off on them.

Be honest. Pace to you is a salsa, isn't it? It also ought to be a famous communications college.

DESTINATION
GUATEMALA

The Official Visitor and Business Guide to Guatemala Compliments
of the Guatemala Chamber of Tourism, Guatemala Tourist Commission and
the Guatemalan Development Foundation

No animal is overlooked when advertising people get involved.
The quetzal bird, the sacred bird of the Mayas and the symbol of
Guatemala, was used on the cover of this visitor's guide.

16

Building *a* Geographic Brand

Travel is one of the heaviest advertising categories. Not only airlines, hotels, and car rental companies, but also cities, states, and countries spend a fortune advertising their facilities and destinations. In our own travels, we often run across many opportunities for PR campaigns that would make much of this advertising unnecessary.

The Guatemala Story

Take Guatemala, for example. What do most Americans know about the country of Guatemala? Not much, except it's a poor country in Central America. That's not much of a reason to go there.

Actually, Guatemala is a country rich in heritage. It was the cultural center of the Mayas, the most advanced civilization in all of North and South America before the arrival of the Spanish. Even today, 44 percent of Guatemala's population of 13 million people is of Mayan descent. Many still speak dialects of the Mayan language.

With mountain ranges as high as 10,000 feet and a culture seemingly unchanged for five hundred years, Guatemala is a tourist paradise. Scattered throughout Guatemala are hundreds of spectacular Mayan ruins. Cities, temples, houses, playing fields, the relics of a glorious past.

Guatemala has everything a world-class tourist destination could want . . . except tourists. Few people know or care about the country.

A PR program focused on Mayan culture could draw tourists to Guatemala. There's one problem, however. Even though Guatemala was the center of Mayan civilization, Mayan ruins are scattered over Belize, El Salvador, western Honduras, and southern Mexico.

Furthermore, how do you solve the confusion problem? In addition to Guatemala, Belize, El Salvador, and Honduras, the Central American Seven include Costa Rica, Nicaragua, and Panama.

How do you solve the confusion problem? You change the name of the country from Guatemala to Guatemaya. This change solves both problems. It preempts the Mayan position and it serves as a memory device to link the Mayas to the country that contains the most spectacular Mayan artifacts. (It also solves a third problem. *Mala* is Spanish for "bad woman.")

A good PR strategy implies a story. The natural reaction of a reporter is to ask, Why did you change the name of the county to Guatemaya?

Our Guatemaya idea was well received among the business community in Guatemala City. They felt it would also solve a political problem with Mayan-speaking people who feel isolated from the Spanish majority. Will it happen? Probably not. You don't see too many quetzal birds going through the eye of a needle either.

The Peru Story

Another country with a tourist problem is Peru. This South American country with a population of 27 million draws only 400,000 tourists a year. (Even Colombia with all its drug problems draws 2 million visitors a year.)

This is odd because Peru is the home of Machu Picchu, which along with the Taj Mahal and the Eiffel Tower is one of the world's three most famous tourist destinations.

Strange as it may seem, Peru needs to move away from its single-minded promotion of Machu Picchu to the promotion of the country as a whole.

If the only tourist attraction in France were the Eiffel Tower, how many tourists would the country attract? Not very many. As attractive as the Eiffel Tower is, it's not enough to justify a trip to France.

The same is true of Machu Picchu. It's a spectacular site, but not enough to justify a trip to Peru.

On the other hand, a country needs a single focus if it is going to attract tourists. The country of France has a single focus, Paris. When you get to Paris, there are a lot of places to visit including the Eiffel Tower.

Where is the Peruvian analogy? Where is the Paris of Peru? We think it's the city of Cuzco. When you get to Cuzco, there are a lot of places to visit, including Machu Picchu.

Could Peru publicize Cuzco as the "Paris of Peru"? Not really. It's a terrible name (sounds like an Italian dessert or worse) and has little recognition around the world. Furthermore, the name does not connote the historical significance of this important city.

What's the real significance of the city of Cuzco? Cuzco was the center of Inca culture, the home of the Incas, using the "king" meaning of the word *Inca*, rather than its ethnic meaning.

What Peru needs to do is to change the name of the city to reflect its true heritage, the home of the Incas. Our suggestion: Ciudad de las Incas.

When you get to Ciudad de las Incas, there are many places to visit, including day trips to spectacular ruins like Machu Picchu.

Both Ciudad de las Incas and Guatemaya provide the hooks to hang publicity programs on. They are also mental hooks that claw their way into tourists' minds. It's not enough for a PR program to produce a pile of clippings. Somehow you have to implant a single motivating idea in the prospect's mind.

What are the chances that Peru will adopt the Ciudad de las Incas strategy? Not great. You don't see too many llamas going through the eye of a needle either.

The Panama Story

Panama, another Central American country, is best known for its canal, yet the country is rather poor, with a per capita GDP of only $7,300. What should the PR posture of Panama be?

Our thought is that Panama should be the world's first "free-trade country." Thanks to the Panama Canal, the country is an ideal assembly and distribution point for shipping products around the world. Although Panama does have free-trade zones, its import tariffs are among the highest in Latin America, ranging from 3 to 50 percent (compared with Mexico's 5 to 20 percent).

But aren't tariffs a political problem? Sure, but you can't isolate PR from politics.

You can't isolate PR from marketing either. The client who says, "We do the marketing, you do the PR," is missing the most important contribution PR can make: changing aspects of the product or service to enhance its publicity potential.

Companies design products to satisfy customers. Rarely do they consider the needs of the media. Yet if a new product does not achieve some media success, it's unlikely to become a marketing success either.

We have seldom worked for a client on a marketing project without suggesting changes. Some minor, most major. And the future success of the brand was more directly related to those strategic changes than it was to all the tactical help we provided.

If you have the right strategy, you can make a lot of tactical errors and still be successful. If you have the wrong strategy, you can be a tactical genius and still be a failure.

Building a City Brand

We met with the tourist promotion people in Sydney, Australia, shortly before the September 2000 Olympics.

The eyes of the world will be on you, we pointed out. This is the perfect time to launch a PR program to promote Sydney.

What's Sydney? If you could answer that question in a single word or concept, you could drive the idea into the minds of the millions of people who will be watching the Olympics as well as the thousands of journalists who will be covering the games.

Cities need a position separate from the country they are located in. Paris is the "City of Lights." New York is the "Big Apple." Rome is the "Eternal City." But what is Sydney?

We set up four criteria for a position for Sydney:

1. It should be a concept that would position Sydney as a "world-class" city along with London, Paris, Rome, New York, and Hong Kong.

2. It should be a concept that has a strong element of believability. People who know Sydney should hear the theme and say, "Yes, Sydney is like that."

3. It should be a concept that is alliterative with the name Sydney. That way the memorability of the idea would be enhanced.

4. It should be a concept that is consistent with the symbol of the city, the Sydney Opera House, one of the five most recognized

buildings in the world. (You can't walk away from what you
already own in the mind.)

Only one idea fits these four criteria. It's simple and obvious. And
with the help of the 2000 Olympics it could have been put in the
minds of millions of people at a very low cost.

"Sydney, the world's most sophisticated city."

If you've been to Sydney, you know that this theme rings true.
Your one objection might be that Australia, with its Outback and its
Crocodile Dundee, doesn't support a sophisticated image. True.

But New York City is not America. And Sydney is not Australia.
Sydney is a second brand, and like all good second brands, should be
divorced from the primary brand.

The problem with treating Australia as a megabrand, master-
brand, or superbrand is that it makes mush out of an individual
brand's position. Megabranding turns powerful brands into "just
another Chevrolet."

On a map, Sydney is inside Australia. But in a mind, "Sydney" and
"Australia" are in two different places. Sydney is sophisticated.
Australia is not. Manhattan is not Peoria.

Building a State Brand

We worked with the state of Missouri to develop a strategy to promote
tourism to the state. Minnesota owns lakes (Land of 10,000 Lakes).
Montana owns sky (Big Sky Country). What could Missouri own?

We decided that Missouri was unique among all the states
because it is at the intersection of the country's two major rivers, the
Missouri and the Mississippi. Literally Missouri is the "river state."

But how to get the media to mention this. Not easy. Our solution was a canoe race from the source of the Missouri River (in Montana) to St. Louis, the point at which the Missouri River flows into the Mississippi.

Coincidentally, this is the route followed (in reverse order) by the Lewis and Clark expedition of 1804. So the media could not only cover the canoe race, but also the famous Lewis and Clark journey. (What the 2000 Olympics could have done for Sydney, the 2004 Lewis and Clark bicentennial could do for the state of Missouri.)

Naturally, the winners would receive their trophies under the Gateway Arch, overlooking both the Missouri and the Mississippi Rivers in downtown St. Louis.

If you want to put "rivers" into the minds of tourists, you have to put "rivers" into the minds of the media first. You also need to be first.

Silicon Valley in San Jose, California, is famous as the home of America's high-tech industry. No less than seventy locations have tried to horn in on its success, including Silicon Beach (Florida), Silicon Alley (New York), Silicon Bayou (Louisiana), Silicon Mountain (Colorado Springs), Silicon Forest (Seattle), Silicon Hills (Austin), Silicon Mesa (Albuquerque), and Silicon Desert (Phoenix).

Which Silicon do you remember? Silicon Valley, of course. Every brand needs its own word and can't get successful by piggybacking on somebody else's word.

If you've ever had an alcohol-related headache.

Skyy managed to secure media attention for its somewhat dubious claim that its vodka is practically hangover-free. Today, Skyy is the second largest superpremium vodka brand.

17

Building *a* Booze Brand

There are exceptions to the general principle that PR builds brands, advertising maintains brands. Altoids was one. Marlboro and Absolut are two more. Marlboro "cowboy" advertising made Marlboro cigarettes famous. Absolut "bottle" advertising made Absolut vodka famous.

If advertising can build brands like Altoids, Absolut, and Marlboro, why can't advertising build your brand? That's a good question, but the answer is good, too. Candy, cigarette, and booze brands receive little publicity. Sure, there's a lot of don't-eat-sweets, don't-smoke-cigarettes, and don't-drink-alcohol publicity, but almost no stories about candy, cigarette, and booze brands.

"There's a great new cigarette on the market called Marlboro Medium" is the headline of a story you will never read in your daily newspaper. Cigarette brands are the kiss of death in the media as well as in the mouth.

Booze, too. With perhaps the single exception of Jack Daniel's, the lack of media coverage of distilled spirits offers an opportunity to use advertising to build a booze brand from scratch. The 1980 launch of Absolut is a classic example. A distinctive bottle, a distinctive name, and distinctive advertising put Absolut into the vodka drinker's vocabulary. "Absolut perfection" read the first advertisement, which had a halo over the Absolut bottle.

Absolut's strategy was good, too. Stolichnaya, the Russian vodka, had made progress with a high-end flanking move against Smirnoff, the longtime vodka leader. But the early eighties brought the height of the Cold War. So Stolichnaya unwisely backed off its Russian heritage, leaving a vacuum for a Swedish product. Furthermore, Stolichnaya is not the easiest name to pronounce, especially after two or three screwdrivers.

A vodka that did manage to find a way to use PR is a brand called Skyy. The brainchild of Maurice Kanbar, Skyy's gimmick is a four-step distillation process that makes the 80-proof vodka so pure it's practically hangover-free or so they say.

Skyy's magic moment was a front-page story in the October 31, 1994, "Marketplace" section of the *Wall Street Journal*: "Hangover-Free Vodka Makes Some Queasy." Skyy went on to become the second-largest superpremium vodka brand in the United States, second only to Absolut. Currently Skyy sells 1.4 million cases annually.

Building a Wine Brand

The wine market in America also illustrates the connection between advertising and PR. Years ago, when few wine stories appeared in the media, you could build a wine brand with advertising. Gallo, Almaden, Inglenook, Taylor, and Paul Masson ("We will drink no wine before its time") were some of the domestic brands running major advertising programs.

On the import side, the leader was Riunite, an Italian Lambrusco wine ("Riunite on ice. That's nice"). Backed by network television commercials, Riunite hit its high-water mark in 1984, when it sold

11 million cases. Cella, Giacobazzi, Bolla, Folonari, Mateus, and Yago Sant'Gria were also big advertisers.

Blue Nun hit it big on radio. With commercials featuring Jerry Stiller and Anne Meara, Blue Nun liebfraumilch captured one-third of the American market for German table wine. In nine years, sales soared more than tenfold to around 1.2 million cases a year.

But as media interest in wine soared, Lambrusco and liebfraumilch got run over by chardonnay and sauvignon blanc. Suddenly the media was talking up the relative merits of vintages, estates, and varietals. The heavily advertised brands got caught in the white glare of publicity and started to fade away.

Wine has entered the PR era. Riunite and Gallo gave way to Robert Mondavi, and Robert Parker Jr. Parker's Publication, *The Wine Advocate,* which accepts no advertising, is the leading authority in the industry. The name of the game today is publicity and a high number from Robert Parker.

Mr. Parker samples 10,000 wines a year, and the effects of his taste buds are global. Prices rise or fall on his judgments. Poor wines score in the 70s, adequate ones in the 80s, and the really good ones in the 90s.

"Once a wine is anointed by the critic Robert Parker," wrote the *New York Times Magazine*, "collectors and wine lovers scramble to purchase whatever they can get their hands on." (Wine drinkers used to drink the label. Today they drink the numbers.)

You can't fight a 75 with an advertising campaign. Nor did advertising have anything to do with Robert Parker's own rise to fame. He correctly predicted that the 1982 Bordeaux vintage would become one of the greatest vintages in wine history. Which it has. The resultant publicity put Robert Parker Jr. and his *Wine Advocate* on the map.

Sure, some wine brands have crawled under Parker's radar screen and established themselves with print advertising campaigns. For the most part, however, these are inexpensive wines appealing to unsophisticated drinkers. (Arbor Mist, Turning Leaf, and Woodbridge are some of the brands.)

The Robert Mondavi Corporation is another wine PR success story. In 1966, Robert Mondavi and his elder son, Michael, built the first new winery in California since Prohibition. (Being first is a typical news hook.)

The key to the success of the firm is Robert Mondavi himself. Now eighty-eight years old, Mondavi is a tireless wine promoter with a single theme: California wines belong in the company of the truly fine wines of the world. *USA Today* called Mondavi "the toast of the wine industry."

Mondavi's company went public in June 1993, always a good idea for generating publicity. But the best idea is Robert Mondavi himself. Every company needs a spokesperson. You can't interview a bottle of wine or a brand of anything. And when the spokesperson has the same name as the name of the company, the publicity potential is doubled.

Publicity is driving the wine business in America. The hot wines today are from Australia, which has captured 11 percent of the American wine market. And Shiraz is the hot Australian grape. Typical newspaper headline: "Awesome Aussie Wines."

The effect of even a little publicity can be awesome. One Sunday evening in 1991, on CBS's *60 Minutes*, Morley Safer reported on the French paradox. Citizens of France and the Mediterranean countries eat fattier foods than we do, smoke and drink more than we do, yet enjoy better cardiovascular health than we do. Why? According to his report, Morley Safer said it's all due to the benefits of drinking red wine. Ever since, sales of red wine have been soaring.

Building a Wine Cooler Brand

Once upon a time, wine coolers were a hot advertising category. The first brand into the pool was California Cooler, whose "crazy" TV spots implied that coolers were for beach bums. Then Bartles & Jaymes hit the airways with award-winning commercials featuring Frank (Bartles) and Ed (Jaymes). The two plain-looking older fellas closed each television spot with the self-effacing tag line "We thank you for your support."

In 1986 alone, Gallo spent an estimated $30 million on Bartles & Jaymes advertising. Canandaigua spent $33 million advertising Sun Country Classic coolers using Ringo Starr as its spokesperson. Seagram also spent a bundle on its Golden Wine Cooler, paying Bruce Willis in the neighborhood of $5 million to tout the product.

As it turned out, 1986 was the high point for wine cooler sales. Under the hot glare of negative publicity they cooled off rapidly. By 1992 they had fallen to half what they were just six years before. And the decline continues today.

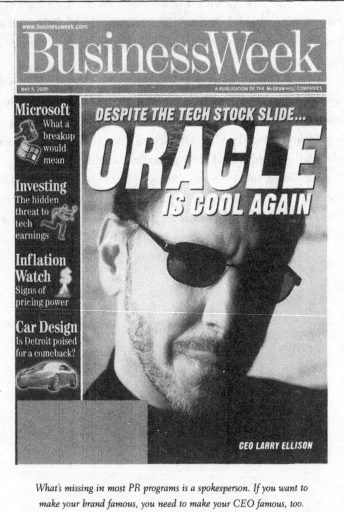

*What's missing in most PR programs is a spokesperson. If you want to
make your brand famous, you need to make your CEO famous, too.
Larry Ellison of Oracle is a typical example.*

18

The Missing Ingredient

The missing ingredient in most marketing programs is the celebrity spokesperson. Products don't create publicity. People do. The media can't interview an automobile, a loaf of bread, or a can of beer. They can only interview a real live person.

Yet many public relations programs are focused on the company and the new product or service the company is introducing. Sure, the new releases might include quotes from various individuals inside and outside the company, but they often don't focus on one individual. "We don't want to give one, single individual the credit for this marvelous new product," goes the refrain. "It was a team effort."

In PR, there is no such thing as a team effort. NBC, CBS, and ABC can't (and won't) interview the team. They want to focus on the individual most responsible for that marvelous new product.

The spokesperson is the face and the voice of the brand. The ultimate success of any PR program depends, to a certain extent, on the effectiveness of the spokesperson. Who should be the spokesperson is a critical decision that should not be made lightly.

Who makes the best spokesperson? In most cases, it is the CEO.

The chief executive officer bears the most responsibility for the success or failure of the brand.

High-tech companies probably understand this PR principle the best. Virtually every high-tech company has a spokesperson who is almost as famous as the company itself.

- Bill Gates and Microsoft
- Larry Ellison and Oracle
- Scott McNealy and Sun Microsystems
- Lou Gerstner and IBM
- Steve Jobs and Apple Computer
- Tom Siebel and Siebel Systems
- Andy Grove and Intel
- Michael Dell and Dell Computer

In the high-tech field, if your CEO is not famous, it's unlikely that your company will be famous and successful, too.

What if your CEO is not good at dealing with the media? The fundamental answer is that you need a new CEO. As a practical matter, a company with a wishy-washy CEO should select the person who will ultimately take over that role and make him or her the company's spokesperson.

Public relations is so important to the long-term success of a company and its brands that the CEO should expect to spend no less than half of his or her time on PR. This is the PR era and it affects the CEO just as much as it affects the rest of the organization.

Look at the big branding successes of the past, and most of them were PR successes. And many of these PR successes were driven by celebrity spokespersons.

- Richard Branson and Virgin Atlantic Airways
- Ted Turner and CNN

- Howard Schultz and Starbucks
- Anita Roddick and The Body Shop
- Donald Trump and the Trump Organization
- Martha Stewart and her magazine, TV show, and product line
- Oprah Winfrey and her magazine and TV show

Building Fast-Food Celebrities

What's true for high tech is also true for fast food. Many of the big fast-food successes have been publicity successes driven by celebrity spokespersons.

- Colonel Sanders and Kentucky Fried Chicken
- Ray Kroc and McDonald's
- Dave Thomas and Wendy's
- Tom Monaghan and Domino's Pizza
- John Schnatter and Papa John's
- Debbie Fields and Mrs. Fields Cookies

One of the problems at Burger King, one of the many problems at Burger King, is the absence of a strong spokesperson. Jeffrey Campbell was on the verge of filling that role until he departed in the wake of the "Herb" disaster.

Herb, the only person in America who had never eaten a Whopper, was the kind of "wild and crazy" advertising that usually appeals to the creative community. Herb went over the edge, however, and was universally condemned.

What happened in fast food is also happening in slow food. You can't open a successful high-end white-tablecloth restaurant without hiring a celebrity chef. Not for attracting customers, but for attracting media attention. (How would a customer know that a certain restaurant has a celebrity chef unless the media reports it?) Charlie Trotter, Wolfgang Puck, Alain Ducasse, Daniel Boulud, Emeril Lagasse, Roy Yamaguchi, and Jean-Georges Vongerichten are some of the celebrity chefs that have made their restaurants famous.

High-end restaurants do little or no advertising. Without favorable publicity they would be without customers. But you don't need continuous publicity. It's like starting a fire. You need an initial burst of publicity to get the blaze going. Once it's lit, once an establishment has a substantial number of core customers, word of mouth will keep it alive and well for a long time with no publicity at all.

Building Financial Celebrities

Another spectacular publicity success is Charles Schwab, who started the first discount brokerage firm. Being first in a new category and having the same name as the name of the firm is an ideal combination for killer publicity. Charles Schwab & Co. rode to the top on a river of publicity about the advantages (and disadvantages) of discount brokerage companies.

Keep in mind that reporters are people, too. They don't want to write or talk about companies until they are already famous. The last thing in the world they want to do is to make your company famous.

What reporters want to talk about are new ideas and new concepts like discount brokerage firms and new California wineries. The unknown company (like Charles Schwab when it was founded) gets a free ride on stories that are essentially about other developments. You feed the media mill by developing strategies that take advantage of this truism. You don't promote yourself. You promote the new idea or new concept you are pioneering. And in the process your company accidentally gets famous, too.

In 1946, Henry and Richard Bloch opened United Business

Company in Kansas City. The fledgling firm provided bookkeeping, collection, management, and tax services to businesses. A small company selling everything under a generic name like United Business has almost no hope of seeing its name in print.

Not until nine years later did the two Bloch brothers make the key decision that made marketing history. They decided to focus on one service only, tax preparation. They also decided to change the name of the company to H&R Block. (They didn't want customers to read the name as "blotch.")

Both moves were brilliant. H&R Block became the first nationwide tax-preparation company, a first that was the source of endless publicity. Every year around April 15, who will the media call for comments about income taxes? H&R Block, of course. Not only the company, but specifically Henry and Richard.

When your name is on the door, you have credibility with the media. This is a trend we heartily endorse. Hiding behind a PR spokesperson is getting to be less of an option for a CEO. Some executives we have worked with worry about the legal consequences of changing their names the way the Bloches did. Social security records, income tax returns, driver's licenses, etc.

Don't worry about any of this. Just use the new name as an aka (also known as) and don't bother to change any of your personal records. In other words, be Block at the office and Bloch at home.

Pizza Celebrities

This history of successful companies is studded with similar examples. Companies that narrowed the focus so they could be first in a new category. And then became successful on a wave of publicity usually generated by the founder.

When Domino's Pizza first got started, Tom Monaghan sold pizza and submarine sandwiches in his store as well as delivered pizzas. He torpedoed the subs and dropped the eat-in service to become a pure pizza delivery chain.

There was no publicity potential in delivering pizzas; most mom-and-pop establishments already did that. The publicity was built around the idea that Domino's was the first pizza chain focused exclusively on home delivery. That was a new idea and the media feasted on it.

When Little Caesars first got started, Michael and Marian Ilitch sold pizza, fried shrimp, fish and chips, and roasted chicken. Only after the Ilitches focused on pizza, and especially take-out pizza, did they develop a reputation for inexpensive food. (Two pizzas for the price of one.)

When Papa John's first got started, John Schnatter sold pizza, cheesesteak sandwiches, submarine sandwiches, fried mushrooms, fried zucchini, salads, and onion rings. Only after Papa John's focused on pizza did the chain start to make progress. But the key decision that led to Papa John's growth was to focus on better ingredients. And to verbalize the idea as "Better ingredients. Better pizza."

The better-ingredients strategy sired many media articles, including a lawsuit from Pizza Hut, which kept the story alive for a number of years. There's nothing like controversy to stir up interest in the media.

Building a Personal Brand

One of the fastest-growing areas is personal PR. If you want to get ahead in a corporation today, you need to be personally "visible." How are you going to do that? By launching an advertising program? Obviously not.

You're going to do that with personal PR. Speeches that get reported in the trade press. Articles that you write for the op-ed pages. Quotes that reporters include in their stories.

In the educational field, the branding of certain institutions has been the work of a small number of high-profile individuals. Michael Porter at Harvard's business school. Philip Kotler at Northwestern's Kellogg business school.

If you are starting a new firm in the fashion industry, it's almost a necessity that you also try to create a celebrity designer. Coco Chanel, Christian Dior, Yves Saint Laurent, Gianni Versace, Calvin Klein, Ralph Lauren, Tommy Hilfiger, for example.

Look at the success of Sean "Puffy" Combs and his clothing company, Sean John. Started two years ago, the company currently does more than $200 million annually in sales. No advertising, of course, but Sean Combs has been spending a bundle on PR and promotion, including a $1.24 million launch of his latest line at Cipriani's catering hall in Manhattan, an event that made the front page of the *New York Times*. The invitations alone are reported to have cost more than $60 each.

*Change is the enemy. By launching New Coke,
the company tried to walk away from ninety-nine
years of cola heritage. Naturally, New Coke was
quickly replaced by Coca-Cola Classic.*

19

Dealing *with* Line Extensions

Those of you who have read our previous books know that we have always taken a strong stand against line extensions. In addition to all the usual reasons, line extensions are media unfriendly.

To an editor or a reporter, a line extension sounds like a me-too product. The media is not interested in your version of somebody else's breakthrough product. The media is interested only if you have a breakthrough product yourself. Some examples:

- Palm, the first handheld computer.
- BlackBerry, the first wireless e-mail device.
- Zip Drive, the first high-capacity external storage system for personal computers.

All three of these "firsts" produced a flood of publicity, which helped establish the three brands as leaders in their field.

Contrast Fat Free Fig Newtons with SnackWell's, the first fat-free cookie. Both were introduced in 1992 by Nabisco, but SnackWell's spawned a sea of publicity while Fat Free Fig Newtons, the line extension, was virtually ignored by the media.

The publicity made SnackWell's a household name, and sales soared three years later to $603 million. By 1995, SnackWell's was one of the ten best-selling grocery items.

Unfortunately sales dropped just as quickly, to $134 million just six years later. Why? Nabisco tacked on a host of line extensions to the brand (none of which generated much publicity), thereby making the same mistake as they had with their Fig Newtons brand. Some of the extensions even included cookies and crackers that weren't fat-free, totally confusing people.

Generating publicity isn't enough, of course. You have to generate the right kind of publicity.

It used to be that any kind of publicity was better than no publicity at all. That was true only when there were few brands on the market and most brands had low awareness levels. Today, hundreds, if not thousands, of brands have awareness levels in the neighborhood of 90 percent. (Look at Interbrand's list of the one hundred most valuable global brands from No. 1 Coca-Cola to No. 100 Benetton. We'll bet you would recognize every single brand and also know what each of the brands stands for.)

The New Coke Calamity

Not all line extensions are publicity disasters. Some line extensions can be publicity successes and product disasters.

When the Coca-Cola Company introduced New Coke, the announcement opened the publicity floodgates. Coke's PR agency at the time estimated that the New Coke introduction produced a billion dollars' worth of free publicity.

Maybe the PR agency meant to say that the billion dollars' worth of free publicity was in Confederate money. Because not a single line of type or a single TV visual was worth a damn to the Coca-Cola brand. The free publicity nearly destroyed the brand.

Less than three months later, Coca-Cola recognized its mistake and backtracked faster than Michael Jackson doing his moonwalk.

Why didn't anyone at Coca-Cola's PR agency say, "Wait a minute. Coca-Cola is the real thing. Its formula, called Merchandise 7X, is so valuable that it's locked in a safe in an Atlanta bank. And you want to change the formula? That's like introducing a new, improved God."

Maybe they did. But our feeling is that the PR people were so focused on the publicity potential of New Coke that they forgot about the brand's position in the mind.

The IBM PC Mishap

If the April 1985 launch of New Coke resulted in a billion dollars' worth of free publicity, then the August 1981 introduction of the IBM PC was good for at least $2 billion worth of free publicity. Another strategic mistake.

The IBM PC was also an exception to the general rule that line extensions dampen the publicity potential. What ignited the publicity engine was that the IBM PC was the first serious sixteen-bit personal computer introduced for the office market. This development was of such importance it overshadowed the weak line-extension name.

By contrast, the Apple IIe, the Commodore Pet, the Radio Shack TRS-80, and all the other personal computers on the market at the time were eight-bit machines designed for the home market.

The impact of the IBM PC launch was enormous. In January 1983, the personal computer was selected by *Time* magazine as "Machine of the Year." For the first time an inanimate object replaced a human being as the magazine's Man of the Year.

Twenty years later, in 2001, the twentieth anniversary of the launch of the IBM PC drew a star-studded crowd, including Bill Gates, and generated millions of dollars' worth of favorable publicity. In the annals of PR history, the launch of the IBM PC will rank right up there with the introduction of the Xerox 914 copier and the Polaroid Land camera. Except for one thing.

Xerox and Polaroid went on to become major brands. The PC did nothing for the IBM brand except lead to large losses and a general retreat from the business personal-computer market. Line extensions tend to do that.

Do you suppose IBM's PR agency recommended a new brand name for the PC before it was launched? Unlikely. But this is exactly the strategic issue that PR firms of the future will have to face.

Don't count on any help from the client's advertising agency. An ad agency generally likes a line extension name because it usually means they get to keep the brand. A new brand name usually means the client has also decided to hire a new ad agency.

Consider the consequences of line extension. When you broaden your line to add dissimilar products, as IBM did with the PC, you lose your focus. You can't advertise or publicize the "line" because the line has nothing in common except a brand name. So you have to advertise or publicize the "extension." That causes confusion. What's an IBM? Is it a mainframe computer or a personal computer?

The Japanese Car Victories

Consider the strategies employed by the Big 3 Japanese automobile companies: Toyota, Honda, and Nissan. All three companies wanted to move up the food chain from small entry-level cars to larger, more expensive cars.

Did Toyota introduce the Toyota BC (for "big car")? Did Honda introduce a Honda Super? Did Nissan introduce a Nissan Ultra? No, all three Japanese automobile companies introduced new brands: Lexus, Acura, and Infiniti.

All three new brands benefited from favorable publicity at the time of their launch. And all three new brands became successful in the U.S. market.

Lexus, in particular. Today Lexus is the largest-selling luxury automobile brand in America, outselling Mercedes-Benz, BMW, Lincoln, and Cadillac.

Now how do you suppose a brand called Toyota BC would have done against competition like Mercedes-Benz, BMW, Lincoln, and Cadillac? Not too well. Selecting the right name is the most important marketing decision you make. The right name leads to favorable publicity and favorable consumer perceptions.

The wrong name leads you on the path to nowhere.

The Road to Disaster Is Paved with Improvements

The more products you hang on a brand name, the weaker the brand name becomes.

In the early eighties, at the time of its PC launch, IBM was the most powerful company in the world. It made the most money and had the best reputation. Yet today the IBM PC is just hanging in there with only 6 percent of the personal-computer market.

Even so, IBM is an exception. The power of the company and the power of the IBM brand have kept its personal-computer hopes alive.

When a line extension is combined with a weaker name, the results are even worse. Where are the personal computers made by AT&T, ITT, Texas Instruments, Atari, Timex, and Mattel? All gone, killed by their line-extension names.

(If you believe in line extensions, and many marketing people do, ask yourself this question: What arguments could I muster to get the Toyota company to change the Lexus brand name to Toyota? Even at this late date, we know what we would say to IBM to try to convince them to market their PC line under a different name. But what would you tell Lexus to convince them to go in the opposite direction?)

Many of America's pharmaceutical companies are finding that a second brand is a much better approach than a line extension . . . even if the drugs are identical. GlaxoSmithKline sells Wellbutrin ($651 million in annual sales) as an antidepressant drug and Zyban ($166 million) as an antismoking drug. Both drugs have exactly the same active ingredient, bupropion hydrochloride.

Eli Lilly has taken the most famous and most successful antidepressant ever, Prozac, which accounts for 30 percent of its total sales, and given it a new name. Lilly has launched a brand-new drug called Sarafem which contains fluoxetine hydrochloride, the generic name for Prozac. Sarafem is being promoted as a treatment for PMDD (premenstrual dysphoric disorder). Launching fluoxetine as a brand-new drug allows Lilly to reach women and their physicians in a way that publicity for the Prozac brand couldn't. Prozac is old news. Sarafem and PMDD are new news.

Merck sells Proscar for treatment of enlarged prostates and Propecia for male-pattern baldness. Both drugs have exactly the same ingredient, finasteride. (If the line-extension crowd got their hands on this product, they would probably use one name with the theme "Head or tail, this is the drug for you.")

Make no mistake about it. Line extensions dampen PR. In spite of the reams of press clippings generated by both New Coke and the IBM PC, it's our belief that line extensions in general dampen publicity coverage, while new brand names accelerate publicity coverage. Suppose IBM had set up a separate division under a different name to launch its first personal computer for the office market. We believe the initial media stories would have been even bigger.

A new name would have given greater emphasis to the people and the facilities behind the new brand. Also, the media would have explored such questions as "Why are you using a new name instead of the IBM name?" (The successful launch of Saturn is a good example of the positive PR a new brand name can generate. "A different kind of company. A different kind of car." Even if Saturn was just another car from General Motors.)

From a strategic point of view, a new name, of course, can help establish the brand as the leader in a new category in the mind.

Advertising people often argue the opposite. They claim it costs too much to try to establish a new brand. What they mean, of course, is that it costs too much to try to establish a new brand *with advertising*.

"It costs too much" is the biggest objection we get when we rec-ommend a new brand name. Companies equate new brands with new advertising programs that cost a fortune.

They shouldn't. For a new brand, advertising has zero credibility. When a brand has established its credentials though publicity, then perhaps advertising can be used. But a new brand should almost never be launched with advertising.

Launching a Small-Car Brand at GM

Look at General Motors' efforts to launch a small-car brand. They first tried it with the Chevrolet Chevette (a typical line extension). After years of mediocre sales, they finally discontinued the Chevette line.

Why would anyone want to buy a small Chevrolet? (It's not the real thing.) Nor did many people want to buy an IBM PCjr, for the same reason. Line extensions are never treated by prospects in isolation. A line extension is always perceived in terms of its relationship to the core brand.

Then Chevrolet moved on to the Chevrolet Geo. With the Geo, they tried exceptionally hard to separate the Geo brand from the Chevrolet brand. The ads said Geo, not Chevrolet. The cars said Geo, not Chevrolet. Unfortunately General Motors sold the Geo in Chevrolet dealerships, so customers automatically said "Chevrolet Geo."

(Lexus, Acura, and Infiniti are perceived as separate brands, but a similar car, the Diamante, is perceived as a Mitsubishi because it is sold in Mitsubishi dealerships. If it looks like a duck and walks like a duck, but it's sold in a chicken dealership, we say it's a chicken.)

Then Chevrolet, or rather General Motors, wised up. GM introduced its smaller Chevrolet as the Saturn. It sold the car in Saturn dealerships and said that it was made by a different kind of car company. Quite naturally the Saturn launch hit the mother lode as far as publicity is concerned and became a big success.

At one point the average Saturn dealer sold more cars per year than the average dealer did with any other automobile brand.

Interestingly enough, Saturn was the only car brand in America that came in just one model. (You could have it in two or four doors or in a station wagon version, but it was essentially the same model, which Saturn calls the S series.)

Then Saturn introduced a larger, more expensive model, the L series. Not a successful introduction and the first step in turning the powerful Saturn brand into a weak brand like Chevrolet.

When you keep a brand like Saturn narrowly focused, you create many publicity opportunities. On the third anniversary of the car's introduction, the company held a "homecoming" for Saturn owners at its Spring Hill, Tennessee, plant. Some 44,000 owners and families showed up. Another 170,000 took part in dealer activities. (Try that with Chevrolet.)

What Saturn did (until they lost their way) is the same thing Harley-Davidson has done over the years—build a loyal group of owners who will sell the brand to their friends and neighbors. HOG, for Harley Owners Group, is the largest motorcycle club in the world, with more than 600,000 members and 1,200 chapters worldwide.

Moving up the Ladder

Why did Saturn introduce a larger, more expensive model, the L series? They wanted to take care of their customers as they grew older, had families, and wanted more luxurious cars. It sounds logical, but it's a flawed strategy.

As a customer moves up the ladder of life, he or she uses brand names as rungs. A single person might buy a Saturn because it's a nice, inexpensive car. When that person gets a raise and a promotion, he or she buys a BMW. When they get married and have kids, they buy a Volvo. When they get divorced, the wife keeps the kids, the house, and the Volvo, and the husband buys a Ferrari.

Brands that don't have a focus don't fit on the rungs of the ladder of life. When you try to appeal to everybody, you wind up appealing to nobody.

Strategy is more important for a PR program than it is for an advertising program. You can always run an ad even if your strategy is atrocious. But PR is different. If the strategy is bad, the publicity is nonexistent.

The Fahrvergnügen Story

A number of years ago, Volkswagen found itself in the same position as Chevrolet. They were trying to market a full line of vehicles with little in common. So the VW advertising agency dreamt up the theme

Fahrvergnügen, which in German means "pleasurable driving experience." With a $100 million advertising budget, the campaign bought a lot of media time and space.

But how much publicity potential is there in *Fahrvergnügen*? Not much.

"What's new about the 1990 Volkswagens?" an automotive reporter might ask.

"They all come with *Fahrvergnügen*."

When asked why the company would sink $100 million into *Fahrvergnügen*, a Volkswagen vice president said, "It is one hundred and eighty degrees different from any price and rebate advertising in the market today."

That may be true, but apparently the campaign didn't do much for Volkswagen sales, which plummeted over the next few years.

There's a lot of *Fahrvergnügen* going on in advertising and marketing circles. New, unusual, creative, and 180 degrees different. Also totally useless for publicity purposes.

PR needs to seize the initiative, to convince companies that brands are built with publicity and not advertising. And then to develop branding strategies that produce effective publicity.

If an advertising agency develops the branding strategy, it's usually *Fahrvergnügen* time. "The advertising business is going down the drain," said David Ogilvy. "It is being pulled down by the people who create it, who don't know how to sell anything, who have never sold anything in their lives . . . who despise selling, whose mission in life is to be clever show-offs, and con clients into giving them money to display their originality and genius."

Fahrvergnügen isn't the only bad name in the marketing arena. There are plenty more milling around the marketplace.

Some categories are serious, some categories are not. A real person with a humorous name like Orville Redenbacher is perfect for a fun food like popcorn.

20

Dealing *with* Names

Nothing in marketing can succeed unless the name is right. The best company, the best product, the best packaging, and the best marketing in the world won't work if the name is wrong. Gablinger's beer, the first light beer, was introduced with award-winning television commercials that received publicity galore. But the brand soon fizzled out.

It didn't taste good, was the conventional wisdom. But taste is in the mind as well as the mouth. (If you've ever fed spaghetti to a blindfolded pledge and told the kid he had to eat worms to get into SAE, you know what we mean.)

Any beer called Gablinger's is not going to taste good . . . especially if it's a diet product. Nor is a beer called Yuengling going to taste good. Was there ever a beer called Yuengling? Sure, see chapter 23.

What's a right name and what's a wrong name? Names cannot be considered in isolation. They have to be looked at in relationship to their categories.

Every Category Is Different

Some categories are funny. Some categories are serious. Popcorn is a funny category and so is the name Faith Popcorn. Beer is a serious category and so is the name Charlotte Beers.

Orville Redenbacher's might be a lousy name for a beer, but it's a great name for a popcorn because popcorn is a funny product and Orville Redenbacher's is a funny name. As a matter of fact, Orville Redenbacher's became the country's largest-selling popcorn brand. (To put the brand into the mind of the popcorn eater, Orville Redenbacher and his wife crisscrossed the continent countless times visiting radio and TV stations, newspapers, and magazines in every major city.)

Redenbacher's big breakthrough came in Chicago when he convinced Marshall Field's to carry his popcorn. To celebrate the occasion, he rented Chicago's Gas Light Club and held a party for food editors. The resulting publicity put Orville Redenbacher's popcorn on the road to national success.

Serious and funny are only two of literally hundreds of attributes a category can have. Categories can be old, young, high-tech, low-tech, high-fashion, low-fashion, masculine, feminine, among the many possibilities. Successful brand names need to connote some essential attribute of the category. (For an energy drink, Red Bull is an excellent brand name.)

Names also imply the opposite. Whom does Slim-Fast appeal to? Slim people or fat people? Obviously Slim-Fast appeals to people who feel they are overweight. In Slim-Fast's case that's acceptable.

And does a motel chain called Quality Inn appeal to people looking for a quality place to spend the night, something on a par with the Ritz-Carlton? Not at all. Quality Inn appeals to people looking for good value for their money.

An Australian entrepreneur was planning to open a chain of high-end clothing stores and sartorial consultants called Esteem. Whom does a store named Esteem appeal to? People with low self-esteem. That's not acceptable. People with low self-esteem will rarely admit the fact.

If You Have a Bad Name, Change It

Ralph Lifshitz changed his name before he got famous. Polo by Ralph Lifshitz doesn't have the same cachet as Polo by Ralph Lauren.

In literature, authors will often give characters a bad name to heighten their negative characteristics. Ebenezer Scrooge in Charles Dickens's *A Christmas Carol*. Willy Loman in Arthur Miller's *Death of a Salesman*. The Grinch in Dr. Seuss's *How the Grinch Stole Christmas*. But why would you accept a bad (or inappropriate) name in a marketing situation?

We once worked with an Italian food company that wanted to develop a new name. After we had selected an appropriate Italian name for the company, we had the nerve to suggest to the CEO and owner that he change his name (which was French) to the new Italian name we had chosen.

Why not? Corporations will spend hundreds of thousands of dollars to develop a brand name and then put that brand name into the mouth of a CEO with a totally inappropriate name.

From a branding point of view, the CEO of a major corporation is in the same position as a television or movie star. A short, simple, easy-to-remember name greatly simplifies the branding process. This is the reason that a substantial percentage of Hollywood legends have manufactured their names:

- Allen Konigsberg became Woody Allen.
- Alphonso D'Abruzzo became Alan Alda.

- Archibald Leech became Cary Grant.
- Cherilyn Shakisian became Cher.
- Tom Mapother became Tom Cruise.
- Bernie Schwartz became Tony Curtis.
- Diane Friesen became Dyan Cannon.
- Margaret Hyra became Meg Ryan.
- Eugene Orowitz became Michael Landon.
- Frances Gumm became Judy Garland.
- Issur Danielovitch became Kirk Douglas.
- Maurice Micklewhite became Michael Caine.
- Michael Guitosi became Robert Blake.
- Shirley Schrift became Shelley Winters.
- Walter Matuschanskayasky became Walter Matthau.

The Operating System of the Mind

Language is the operating system of the mind. No word is ever accepted on its own merit. Every sound, every syllable, carries its own baggage, which is sometimes positive, sometimes negative, sometimes neutral. If you want to create a favorable impression in the mind, you have to use words that reflect the perception you are trying to create.

Donald Trump's family name was Drumpf. Would Drumpf Towers have sold as well as Trump Towers? We don't think so. Neither would Lipshitz Towers. Or Bin Laden Towers, for that matter.

Pulte Homes, the nation's second-largest homebuilder, called us to inquire about a branding project. It's an enormous opportunity, we were told, 60 percent of homeowners can't identify the builder of their house.

We could understand that. If our home were built by Pulte, we wouldn't want to remember the name either. Change your name.

Not a chance. (The founder's name is Pulte.) So the company is currently spending $30 million a year on advertising, including a float in Macy's Thanksgiving Day parade and television ads. The agency is Bcom3 Group's D'Arcy Masius Benton & Bowles. (At least they hired an ad agency that can't complain about using a bad name.)

The Saudi Binladin Group, one of the world's largest construction companies, has recently been interviewing PR firms. If your firm got the Saudi Binladin account, what would be the first thing you would suggest?

Many companies have a tin ear when it comes to their own brands. Why would the Kellogg Company market sauces and gravies under the LeGout name? Don't they realize the customer might assume that LeGout sauces are a little too rich?

Then there's a company named Sappi, which calls itself "the word for fine paper." We though Sappi was the word for foolish people.

Building a Beer Brand

We once did work for the Pittsburgh Brewing Company, whose major brand is Iron City beer. The client wanted to take the brand national. Naturally we said no.

Why can't Iron City become a national brand? brewery management wanted to know. If Rolling Rock, brewed in Latrobe, Pennsylvania, can become a successful national brand, why can't Iron City?

Iron City is not Rolling Rock. The beers might be similar, but the names are different. Rolling Rock rolls off the tongue like a refreshing waterfall, while Iron City conjures up mostly negative thoughts of steel and despair. How do you explain to someone who lives in Pittsburgh that "rusty beer" won't sell in Palo Alto or Palm Beach? It's not easy.

(How do you explain to someone who lives in Green Bay, Wisconsin, that those cheesehead hats are unlikely to become a fashion item?)

And why do you think Schlitz is no longer the best-selling beer in America, as it once was? Could it be the name? When Al was barely old enough to drink, the guys in the tavern had a bit of doggerel that went, "It may be Pabst in the glass, but it's Schlitz in the pants."

Horse Mackerel and Other Loser Names

Tuna fish used to have an Iron City name. It was called horse mackerel. And canola oil was once called rapeseed oil. If you have a horse-mackerel or rapeseed name, change it. Names make a difference, especially in PR, where the message is totally out of your control.

A number of years ago, miniature chickens were promoted as "Rock Cornish game hens." Recently the California Prune Board won permission from the government to start calling prunes "dried plums." But the change is likely too late to improve the prune's reputation. The prune name is already firmly established in the mind, and changing a mind is a difficult, if not impossible, thing to do.

The time to change a name is before it makes it into the mind. The Chinese gooseberry was unknown in the United States until an importer changed its name to kiwifruit. (Some foods have dual names, such as the hazelnut, also known as the filbert, and chickpeas, also known as garbanzos. When was the last time you ordered a filbert-flavored coffee? The better names are much more widely used.)

A decade ago, General Motors chose Impact as its brand name for a new electric car. Impact is not a good choice for an automobile brand because the name conjures up the wrong image. "What, was Fiery Ball of Death already taken?" quipped Jay Leno.

F. Scott Fitzgerald wanted to call his book *Trimalchio* until his editor talked him into calling it *The Great Gatsby*. The heroine's name in *Gone With the Wind* was originally Pansy O'Hara until an editor changed it to Scarlett.

Alice Rosenbaum changed her name to Ayn Rand. Faith Plotkin changed her name to Faith Popcorn.

Palm Island in the Grenadines used to be Prune Island. Paradise Island in the Bahamas used to be Hog Island.

When you give your brands powerful names, the names themselves help produce effective publicity. Wilson called its new tennis racquet the Hammer, and every serious tennis player had to have one. Callaway called its oversize driver the Big Bertha, and every serious golfer had to have one. Nike called its running shoe Air Max, and every serious runner had to have one.

An Airline or a Flightless Bird?

Why would you call an airline that flew up and down the east coast of the United States Kiwi International Airlines? A kiwi is a flightless bird that lives in New Zealand; it doesn't make sense as the name for an airline brand in America.

When Kiwi went bankrupt and became a flightless airline in 1996, four years after its hatching, its CEO blamed the fallout from the ValuJet crash and the government's increased scrutiny of start-up airlines. No mention was made of its flightless-bird name.

In 1994 Kiwi was honored as the best domestic airline by readers of *Condé Nast Traveler*, perhaps the most authoritative publication in the travel industry. How could the best domestic airline go broke just two years later?

Brands are built in the mind, primarily with publicity. What do you suppose is the first question a reporter might ask Kiwi management? Why did you give a New Jersey airline a New Zealand name?

(ValuJet, we should remind you, is still flying, but under a different name, AirTran. Would an AirTran-type name have saved Kiwi? We think so.)

The Product or the Name?

To most CEOs we have met, names don't matter. It's always the product, the price, the service, the distribution. Yet names can often make a striking difference. Master Charge (before its name change to MasterCard) was the leading credit card company in the country. BankAmericard was in second place. Then in March 1977, BankAmericard changed its name to Visa.

Today Visa has almost twice the market share of MasterCard, and the new name is given much of the credit. For one thing, many banks balked at using the name of one of their rivals (BankAmerica). For another, the Visa name has the glamour and international cachet that the MasterCard name does not.

Many companies shy away from changing their names because they think it's too expensive. When someone suggests a name change, the first thing that comes to mind is an expensive advertising campaign.

Why spend the money on advertising a name change when publicity can do a better job for a lot less money? When Philip Morris Companies Inc. announced that it was going to change its name to Altria Group, Inc., the heavy lifting was done by publicity. Altria ads were mostly ignored. Who is going to read a self-serving advertisement entitled "When a company outgrows its name"?

Why the Altria name? "Derived form the Latin *altus*, meaning high," states the ad, "Altria symbolized our company's constant desire to reach ever higher—a philosophy that has always guided our decisions." Not mentioned anywhere in the Altria advertisement were the words *tobacco* or *cigarettes*. (The obvious reason for the name change is to move away from cigarettes.)

But *tobacco* was all over the place in the news stories about the same event. "Company Would Divert Attention from Tobacco," said the headline in the *New York Times*. If all advertising were as blunt, honest, and straightforward as the news stories you see, read, or hear in the media, we suppose advertising might have some credibility. But what effect can an honest advertisement have in a sea of subterfuge?

"Liars, when they speak the truth," wrote Aristotle, "are not believed." Every advertisement you run is judged not by the weight of what you say but by the weight of all the other advertisements that have ever run. (It may be a duck, but it lives in a chicken environment.)

A New Name for Andersen Consulting

Changing a name often creates opportunities to develop favorable publicity. As a consequence of its divorce from the Arthur Andersen accounting firm, Andersen Consulting was forced to change its name. An employee contest came up with the winning name, Accenture, a telescoping of the term *accent on the future*.

But where is the publicity potential of a name like Accenture? As far as the media is concerned, Accenture is just another manufactured corporate name along with Altria, Avaya, Aventis, Agilent, Azurix, etc.

A good name has story value. It suggests an idea that reporters can explore. Where is the story value in "accent on the future"? What corporation doesn't spend endless hours studying, planning, and worrying about the future? Accenture sounds like just another million-dollar-corporate-identity-firm concoction.

Finding a name with story value usually means finding an issue that differentiates a company from all of its competitors. That's actually easy to do for Andersen Consulting.

Unlike its competitors (IBM, EDS, KPMG Consulting, and others), Andersen Consulting recruits the bulk of its employees directly from college and trains them in the "Andersen way" at a facility in St. Charles, Illinois. What name would exploit this differentiating idea?

St. Charles Consulting is the obvious answer. When a reporter asks, "Why did you call the company St. Charles Consulting?" the answer effectively positions the new company. "We call ourselves St. Charles Consulting to call attention to the fact that the bulk of our employees have been extensively trained in the St. Charles way at our facility in St. Charles, Illinois."

Don't misunderstand. With a less-than-ideal name, the sheer size and weight of a company like Accenture will make it successful. When you're a billionaire, or a billionaire company, a missed opportunity is nothing to cry about. Our concern is with the smaller company that blindly follows the Accenture path.

"If Accenture can, why can't we?" That might be the attitude of an average-size company. But with a smaller company, the choice of a new name can be a life-or-death decision. A smaller company is not Accenture, so it needs a name that has the best chance of earning favorable publicity.

The biggest mistake a mini-corporation can make is emulating the mega-corporation. We frequently hear, "Why can't we sell everything? Wal-Mart does." Our answer is always the same: "You're not Wal-Mart."

When Jack Welch took over as CEO in 1981, General Electric was already No. 1 or No. 2 in most of the businesses the company participated in. How many companies can benefit from emulating GE? Very few.

Someone asked Babe Ruth what he did to prepare for a ball game.

Well, said the Babe, I hit the hot spots, stay out till 2 A.M., have a half quart of whiskey, and enjoy myself.

Before you are tempted to do the same thing, ask yourself, "Am I Babe Ruth?" Or Wal-Mart? Or General Electric? Staying on top of the mountain and getting to the top of the mountain are two different things.

PART THREE

A New Role
for Advertising

To get more intimate with your partner, whisper those three little words.

"See your doctor."

If you and your partner are experiencing a decline in sexual activity, it may be the result of erection difficulties, such as erectile dysfunction (ED). Fact is, ED is a common health condition. It can be caused by factors such as high blood pressure, high cholesterol, diabetes, even stress. Fortunately, there is a proven treatment—VIAGRA. **More than 9 million men** have already turned to it.

So talk to him. He needs your support because it's not just about sex. It's about his health, too.

For more information, call 1-888-4VIAGRA or visit www.viagra.com.

VIAGRA®
(sildenafil citrate) tablets

Join the millions. Have him ask his doctor about a free sample.

VIAGRA is indicated for the treatment of erectile dysfunction. Remember that no medicine is for everyone. If you use nitrate drugs, often used to control chest pain (also known as angina), don't take VIAGRA. This combination could cause your blood pressure to drop to an unsafe or life-threatening level.
Discuss your general health status with your doctor to ensure that you are healthy enough to engage in sexual activity. If you experience chest pain, nausea, or any other discomforts during sex or an erection that lasts longer than 4 hours, seek immediate medical help. The most common side effects of VIAGRA are headache, facial flushing, and upset stomach. Less commonly, bluish vision, blurred vision, or sensitivity to light may briefly occur.

With no consumer advertising at all, Viagra became a successful worldwide brand almost overnight. Today, however, Viagra spends $90 million a year on ads like this.

21

Maintaining
the Brand

Advertising is not brand building. That's the role and function of PR. Advertising is brand maintenance.

Advertising's role is the continuation of public relations by other means. But just because the means change doesn't mean the policy of the public relations program should change. Advertising should continue to reinforce PR ideas and concepts.

A brand is born with the capability of creating "news." This is the essence of a new brand. But what happens when a brand grows up? It runs out of its publicity potential.

The media loved Starbucks, Viagra, and PlayStation, but you seldom see stories about these brands anymore. They are yesterday's news.

Sooner or later, every brand runs up against a PR brick wall. No matter what you do, you cannot tempt the media to reprise the story of the brand. This is the time to switch the strategy of the brand from PR to advertising.

Fishing Expeditions

But what kind of advertising? Here is where many companies go off course. Instead of running advertising reinforcing what the publicity has already produced, the brand owners go on fishing expeditions. They run advertising that explores new markets, new benefits, and/or new demographic segments.

- Volvo owned "safety," so they are using advertising to try to drive the brand over to the performance side of the market. They even introduced the S-70 line of sporty coupes and convertibles. A convertible Volvo is an oxymoron.
- H&R Block owned "tax preparation," so they are using advertising to try to move the brand over to one that also offers "financial services."
- Heineken owned "expensive imported" beer for the older crowd, so they are using advertising to try to capture the younger, hip crowd.

These and other brands might register some successes with such strategies, but the successes are likely to be short-term. Momentum in marketing assures the near future will be similar to trends in the past. When a rocket runs out of fuel, it continues its upward ascent until its momentum loses the battle with gravity. Then it falls from the sky.

Not Your Father's Oldsmobile

The classic example of an expansion failure is Oldsmobile. Who can forget "This is not your father's Oldsmobile"? This was an advertising-driven marketing program that achieved phenomenal levels of awareness.

"This is not your father's Oldsmobile" has all the ingredients of what brand-building advertising is supposed to be about. It had a memorable slogan, it had "talk value," and it had a motivating reason for the younger crowd to buy an Oldsmobile.

Oldsmobile had just introduced its Aurora model and later its Alero and Intrigue models, performance cars with head-turning styling that definitely had appeal to younger people.

In spite of the campaign, Oldsmobile sales went down. And even more embarrassing, the average age of an Oldsmobile buyer went up.

You can't fight a perception with advertising. You can't even fight a perception with truth. (Even the Oldsmobile name contributed to the perception that the car was for older people. Why would a young person want to drive an Olds?)

Broadening vs. Deepening

One of the classic ways to use advertising is for the purpose of "broadening the brand."

- Orange juice is not just for breakfast anymore. Florida Citrus Commission.
- We're not just an orange juice company anymore. In addition to orange juice, Tropicana now sells grapefruit juice, apple juice, grape juice, cranberry juice, fruit punch, lemonade, and Twister juice beverages.
- We're not just for kids anymore. "Come be a kid again" is the theme of a Walt Disney World campaign that urges older people

to visit the parks. If you don't have kids, why would you want to visit Walt Disney World?

- We're not just for the younger generation anymore. "Gotta have it" was the theme of a short-lived Pepsi-Cola program featuring such older swingers as Yogi Berra, Jimmy Connors, and Dr. Joyce Brothers.

"The one drawback of Pepsi advertising in the past has been a little too much focus on youth," said the ad agency executive responsible for the program. "We could have made greater gains had we expanded our horizons to cast a wider net and catch more people rather than kids only."

It's a "Who's going to bell the cat?" situation. The strategy makes sense, but it won't work because it depends on advertising to do a job that advertising cannot do.

Advertising cannot change minds. Advertising cannot move brands from one position to another inside a mind. Advertising cannot replace an existing brand in the mind with a new brand. All of these jobs are outside the scope of an advertising solution.

Advertising can only deal with an existing perception in the mind. Advertising can only deepen that perception, not change it or modify it or broaden it. Skillfully handled, however, that deepening strategy can pay big dividends.

Accept What You Already Own in the Mind

The ground rules for a successful advertising program start with acceptance. Accept what your brand already owns in the mind and move on from there.

Furthermore, you will usually find that a brand's current market share is only a fraction of its potential market share.

Because Volvo owns the safety position, the brand is widely known as "the soccer mom's car." How many soccer moms are driving in America? Perhaps 5 million. Since Volvo is currently selling just over 100,000 cars a year, it's obvious that the brand is far from dominating the soccer-mom market.

We're not suggesting that Volvo literally run soccer-mom spots, although that might be one possibility. Rather, Volvo should focus its advertising on the "safety" position it already owns. This has four benefits: (1) It reminds prospects of the primary benefits of buying a Volvo. (2) It educates new buyers who might just be coming into the market. Over time, people grow up. (3) It deepens the market by making safety a more important reason for buying a car. Over time, people might become more aware of the carnage that takes place on American highways. More than one hundred people die every day. (4) It protects the brand from competitors who might otherwise want to try to establish a safety position.

Reminding, educating, deepening, and protecting are four good reasons for running an advertising program that reinforces an existing perception in the mind. Especially when you compare it with the alternative, running an advertising program that tries to change an existing perception. History shows the latter approach, because of advertising's lack of credibility, just won't work.

Take H&R Block, which is trying to expand into financial planning, home mortgages, brokerage services, and even private wealth management. Will customers of Merrill Lynch, Charles Schwab, or Citibank decide to go to H&R Block for financial advice because they see a television commercial on the subject? We think not.

On the other hand, tax preparation remains pretty much an untapped market. H&R Block helps prepare only 14 percent of the 132 million tax returns filed annually. (This includes its owned and franchised offices and its on-line and software products.)

H&R Block could benefit from "deepening" the brand to attract more of the 114 million tax returns it is missing.

Take Heineken. Here is a brand that used to call itself "the largest-selling imported beer in America." No longer. That position is now owned by Corona Extra. While it was chasing the hip crowd, Heineken lost its leadership position. What does Heineken stand for today? The brand is in danger of becoming "just another beer."

Reinforcing a Leadership Position

Advertising is particularly appropriate when you want to reinforce a leadership position. And when you own the leadership position, you generally want to reinforce it.

Leadership alone is one of the primary objectives of any marketing program. It's why you want to create a new category (so you can start the brand from day one as the leader). It's why you want to be the first brand in the new category (so you have a head start on your competition). It's why you want to promote your leadership (so prospects assume that your brand must be the best because everybody knows the better product will win in the marketplace).

The advantage of leadership as an advertising theme is its credibility. Let's say your brand has a number of attributes you could advertise: performance, durability, ease of use, and leadership. Performance, durability, and easy of use are matters of opinion. Your competitors' advertising might challenge you on these very issues. Leadership is not debatable. There can be only one sales leader in beer, in tires, in Internet service, in ketchup: Budweiser, Goodyear, AOL, and Heinz. Each of these brands, to one extent or another, has run advertising extolling its leadership.

Leadership has credibility. Leadership also has the implied benefit of "betterness." AOL must have the better internet service because they are the leader.

Even better is to connect your leadership to a specific benefit that has already been implanted in prospects' minds via publicity. America Online is widely known as the Internet service provider for beginners. "The Internet on training wheels" is how the computer nerds bad-mouth AOL.

So AOL's advertising takes advantage of both its leadership and its presumably negative perception. "So easy to use, no wonder it's No. 1."

Coca-Cola's logical advertising slogan ("the real thing") combines the implication of leadership with the attribute of "original." Everything else is an imitation of Coke.

The Creativity Issue

Why doesn't Coca-Cola resurrect "the real thing"? Advertising people always fight this type of program because "it's not creative."

Creativity itself is the biggest obstacle toward establishing a new role for advertising. Literally every advertising strategy we have ever developed for any client we have ever worked with (and there have been hundreds) has been resisted by some advertising people because the strategy "wasn't creative."

Years ago, we worked for a double drive-through hamburger chain called Rally's that competed with the single drive-through units at McDonald's and Burger King. Our strategy was to focus on speed: the sixty-second hamburger, or something like that.

No, said the famous copywriter who was serving as the client's creative consultant, that's not creative. It's too obvious. We should focus on getting the order right.

Where's the credibility in that? we asked. You can see why the client's stores are fast. They're small and they're totally dedicated to takeout. Furthermore, Rally's has two drive-through windows instead of one. If speed wasn't going to be the primary benefit, why did they choose Rally's as the brand name?

We lost this argument, and many others, to opponents who invoked the word *creativity* to justify another point of view.

No Need for Creativity

Any brand considering an advertising program doesn't need "creative" advertising. If it does, then the brand should use PR instead.

You "create" brands by PR. You maintain brands with advertising.

Advertising didn't create the Goodyear brand, but it's doing a great job of maintaining the brand.

Advertising is the cheerleader that repeats words and ideas that already exist in the mind. The objective of an advertising program is to bring these words and ideas to the surface and to make them resonate in the mind.

The advertising agency creative director who brings an original cheer to the big game is going to be disappointed with the crowd's reaction.

"What the hell was that all about?" is a typical reaction to most television commercials. The creativity gets in the way of the true function of advertising, which is not to inform or communicate. The true function of advertising is to reinforce an existing perception in the mind.

"Tylenol is the pain reliever hospitals use most." It must be better than aspirin or Advil, thinks the prospect, otherwise hospitals, the most informed institutions in the world of medicine, wouldn't use so much Tylenol. Creative? No. Effective? Yes. In drugstores today, Tylenol is the largest-selling single brand.

Look at movie ads. If you are a copywriter on a movie account at an advertising agency, you have nothing to do. Invariably all the copy in a movie ad is taken strictly from movie reviews. Why is this? The movie studio has no credibility with the public, who will believe only what the reviewers have to say about a film.

The wine drinker who has read all about Australian wines in the media is going to respond favorably to a Rosemount ad that says, "The No. 1 selling Shiraz in America." Forget the kangaroos and the koalas. Rosemount runs ads to solidify its position, not to exercise its creativity.

Contrast Rosemount with Budweiser. Dogs, frogs, lizards, and ferrets have followed Budweiser beer as it has steadily declined in popularity. Beer sales might be down, but creative awards are up as the Bud ads continue to collect barrels of silverware.

What legitimate, credible ideas are in the mind of the beer drinker when you mention Budweiser? The only animals that come to mind are the Clydesdale horses, once used to pull Budweiser beer wagons. And the only motivating idea associated with Budweiser is "king of beers."

(Miller Brewing has been running a holiday television commercial for the past few years featuring a couple riding on a horse-drawn sleigh. Until the final scene, when the Miller logo appears, many people think this is a Budweiser spot.)

Budweiser should run advertising with the theme "king of beers," and it should use the beer wagon and the Clydesdales to reinforce its heritage as one of the oldest, best-known, best-loved breweries in the country. Once in a while, Anheuser-Busch does run a Budweiser commercial using the Clydesdales, including a recent Super Bowl spot. According to an *Adweek* poll of 5,260 people, the Clydesdale spot was the best-liked 2002 Super Bowl commercial by a wide margin.

You might think that beer drinkers connect Budweiser with frogs, lizards, and the latest hip expression, "Whassup?" But they don't. They connect "Whassup?" and the frogs and the lizards with Budweiser advertising. There is a difference.

The Dilemma of Creative Advertising

More than forty years ago, famed researcher Alfred Politz pointed out the pitfalls when clients demand creative advertising. In an article entitled "The Dilemma of Creative Advertising," Politz writes, "It is unfortunate, but not surprising, that the creative man now diverts his efforts from making the product interesting to making the advertising interesting. Ultimately he is no longer selling the product to the consumer, but selling the advertising to his client."

As long as agencies are selling advertising to clients, instead of products to consumers, the pressure will be on for "creative advertising." It has to be new, it has to be different, and it has to be original. Exactly those attributes that divorce the advertising from the product itself.

What needs to be new, different, and original is the product, not the advertising. These are the attributes that capture the media's attention.

Actually, we'll take that back. What needs to be new, different, and original is the perception of the product. And this is the task of the PR person. How do we take a product or service and skillfully position the brand so it achieves the perception of being new, different, and original?

In other words, the creativity belongs in the PR, not in the advertising. Advertising's job, when it is used, is to reinforce the ideas planted in the mind with the publicity.

No Return on Investment

If an emphasis on creativity is the biggest advertising mistake you can make, the second-biggest advertising mistake you can make is looking for an ROAI, or return on advertising investment.

The days are long since gone when you could spend a million dollars on advertising and increase your profits by a million dollars in the same year. Yet some advertising advocates believe in the ROAI approach. However, they look at advertising as an investment that will pay off sometime in the future, rather than during the current year. If we spend a million this year, it might pay off in the next five years or so.

Some advocates have even gone so far as to recommend treating advertising as a capital expense, the same way that some companies treat their research and development expenditures. They recommend capitalizing the advertising investment on the balance sheet.

No matter how many times you spin the numbers, it's hard to prove the ROAI theory. Advertising does not generally pay for itself. These days, most advertising agencies rely more on the "belief" approach. If you believe in advertising, then you should support a substantial advertising budget. Heaven help you in corporate America today if you are an advertising infidel.

In our scheme of things, advertising is not an investment that is likely to pay dividends. Advertising is insurance. That is, advertising protects a brand from competitive attacks. Advertising is the price you pay to maintain your brand's position in the mind. Brand maintenance rather than brand building.

On the balance sheet, advertising is more like maintenance than it is like research and development. Without the advertising expenditures, the value of the brand would depreciate. Advertising is not going to pay off in the future. It's going to protect the brand today.

The best advertising programs have an "I knew that before, but I'm glad you reminded me" quality. "A diamond is forever," DeBeers' long-running campaign, is in that category. Rather than being information-laden, the best advertising programs are usually emotion-laden (the cheerleading analogy).

If advertising is insurance, what's the ROI of insurance? If you spent $1,000 on life insurance this year, what did you get for your money? Nothing, of course, unless you died. Insurance is an accepted business expense even though it doesn't pay dividends. Why not advertising?

One way the ROAI crowd tries to justify advertising investments is to spend the advertising money on line extensions. In some product categories, most notably food, you seldom see any advertising pushing the basic brand.

What you do see is an endless number of line extensions. New flavors, new sizes, new ingredients, new categories. Crest toothpaste, Crest toothbrushes, Crest mouthwash. Crest plus Scope. And the latest, Crest Whitestrips.

How much to spend on advertising once a brand is established is a delicate decision. You want to spend enough to protect the brand from competition, even though this might mean no increase at all in your market share.

In some cases, you might spend nothing at all and let the brand die a natural death. This is especially true in categories that are declining in sales and don't have much of a future.

How much should Smith-Corona have spent on typewriter advertising in the early days of the personal computer? Nothing.

No Chance of Fighting a Trend

Advertising cannot fight a trend.

If the tide is against you, the best strategy is to let your brand drown and launch a new brand to take advantage of the next wave. Smith-Corona should have launched a personal computer with a different brand name.

When the blue jean market suffered a downturn, Levi Strauss launched the Dockers brand of casual slacks. Today, Dockers is a

billion-dollar worldwide brand. To publicize the brand and to acceler-
ate the trend toward more casual dress in business situations, Levi
Strauss invented Dress Down Fridays. The company even sent Dress
Down Friday press kits to corporate human-relations directors.

When you select a new name for your second brand, beware of
research. You can't evaluate the power of a second brand "before the
fact." Before the launch of Lexus, if you had asked people if they
would rather buy a Toyota Ultra or a Lexus, guess which brand they
would have preferred by a wide margin. The Toyota Ultra, of course.

People prefer names they know to names they don't know. The
power of publicity made Lexus the brand it is today.

ROCKY MOUNTAIN HIGH

Adolph Coors

Sold only in the West, Coors beer
is smuggled to the East. Henry Kissinger drinks it.
So does Paul Newman,
though he would abhor the Coors family's politics.

By Grace Lichtenstein

Equal Employment Opportunity Commission charging the company with race and sex discrimination.

In many ways, Coors is the perfect product of the American free-enterprise system to which its top officials regularly pay homage. Since Adolph Coors began bottling the brew in 1873, the operation has expanded into a $585 million business, employing some 7,500, most of them in the brewery and related facilities sprawled on 3,100 acres in Golden. It has climbed from 12th in national sales in 1965 to fourth (behind Budweiser, Schlitz and Pabst), even though it is distributed in only 11 Western states while its competitors are selling throughout the country. It is the leader in all but one of its states, the exception being Texas (where it is not distributed in all areas). Moreover, it has captured the No. 4 spot with a bare minimum of paid advertising. Over the years, the company has

acquired its own barley fields, rice-milling facilities, construction crew, aluminum-can-manufacturing plant, and trucks, so that it relies on the outside world for as little help as possible. Coors even owns some natural-gas reserves to supply its plants with fuel.

But it is not so much the product as the mystique surrounding it that is fascinating. It seems to have won a reputation as the elixir of beers, the brew of Presidents, a prize to be smuggled into the East the way Americans abroad used to smuggle in contraband copies of Henry Miller's novels. Paul Newman, the king of beer-drinking actors, is said to require Coors on ice at all his movie sets. Henry Kissinger regularly brought cases back to Washington each time he made a trip to California. Secret Service agents were forbidden to bring extra crates aboard Federal planes after one agent was discov-

ered to have loaded 38 cases onto a recent flight from the West Coast.

Bootleggers from New Jersey to Tennessee regularly sell cases of Coors for as much as $15—about three times the Colorado retail price. (And three times what a New Yorker may pay for that favorite of Met fans, Schaefer.) Obviously, Coors must be a magic potion, not simply a fermented blend of barley malt, rice, hops and "Pure Rocky Mountain Spring Water." What accounts for the magic?

"I frankly can't explain it," says Ernest Pyler, editor of Brewers Digest. "Coors by brewing standards is a good beer, but so are many others. I think it's mostly because of its unavailability." Joe Nazzaro, a bartender from Connecticut who works at the Ute City Banque restaurant in Aspen, remarks: "It's funny. I go home to Connecticut; it's a big deal to bring my father a couple of cases of

Coors. But out here I don't think twice about it."

Neither do many Westerners. Even though they chug-a-lug gallons of the stuff, it is probably because Coors is cheap and plentiful. I've never seen any of the local folks fuss when a bar is out of Coors; they simply order something else. Montanans, who are outside the Coors territory, would no more pay $15 for a case of Coors than they would for a case of Dr. Pepper. "Are you kidding?" laughed a friend from Billings. "For $15 I could buy me a nice big bottle of Haig & Haig Pinch."

Another explanation has been offered by William K. Coors, chairman of the board and second-oldest son of Adolph Coors 3d, who followed his father as head of the company. (The oldest son, Adolph 3d, was murdered in 1960 after being kidnapped, apparently for ransom.) "There's no mystique about Coors's popularity," Bill Coors told one interviewer. "It tastes better than other beers, that's all."

Taste, of course, is a subjective thing. Some Coors detractors who like to make fun of Easterners' silly addiction say that what makes Coors distinctive is its lack of taste. I think they may be right, although I'm hardly a beer connoisseur. I had never drunk beer until a few years ago, when a skiing companion in Utah invited me to join in his ritual of burying a can of Coors in snow before hitting the slopes, then digging it out at the end of the day for a cold pick-me-up. The very pleasure of Coors (and my thirst after a day of skiing) made it easy for a nondrinker like me to acquire the taste.

Coors is a light-bodied beer, meaning it is brewed with less malt, fewer hops and more rice than beers with a tangy taste. Compared with Heineken's or other more full-bodied foreign beers, Coors does seem almost flavorless and it is this quality that could account for its popularity among young people just starting to get acquainted with the pleasures of beer drinking. A few locals scoff at Coors, calling it "Colorado Kool-Aid." But the fact is that, according to Ernest Pyler, "if you conducted a blindfold test of the four leading beers, the chances of picking out Coors would be minimal." Indeed, one national newspaper conducted an informal test among eight beer

*The magic moment for Coors was this highly favorable article
in* The New York Times Magazine. *Then Coors went
off course with product line extensions and
a brewery line extension.*

22

Keeping On Course

Many brands get launched in a blaze of publicity that establishes ideas and concepts about the brand in the prospect's mind. Then the advertising department deliberately goes out and launches an advertising campaign that clearly contradicts what the brand stands for.

Losing the way, courtesy of the advertising department, is much more common than you might think.

Going Off Course at Coors

No beer brand, for example, has ever received as much publicity as Coors. "Rocky Mountain High," said the headline of a 1975 article in the *New York Times Magazine*.

"The most chic brew in the country. Henry Kissinger drinks it. So does Paul Newman," reported the *New York Times Magazine*. This was the magic moment that should have taken Coors to the top of the beer ladder. But it didn't.

Encouraged by its publicity windfall, Coors used advertising to roll out the brand to the national market. Unfortunately, Coors advertising cut the chic right out of the brand. It forgot to mention what was prominently printed on the label, "American's Fine Light Beer." In fact Coors was the country's first light beer. (Regular Coors beer has fewer calories than Michelob Light.)

Then Coors undermined its light-beer heritage by watering down the core product with a brand called Coors Light. (Would the Jack Daniel Distillery have introduced Jack Daniel's Light?)

Then Coors undermined its Rocky Mountain spring water heritage by opening a second brewery in Virginia. Coors had spent more than one hundred years telling beer drinkers that Rocky Mountain spring water was the special ingredient that gave Coors its unique flavor. Then, to save on transportation costs, Coors decided to use Elkton, Virginia, spring water to brew Coors beer.

How special could Rocky Mountain spring water really be if Coors brews beer for its East Coast drinkers without it?

Going Off Course at Coca-Cola

Coca-Cola copied Coors. Like Coors, the Coca-Cola company has consistently ignored its history, its heritage, and its mystique in favor of clever, creative advertising. Here is a brief history of the main themes of Coca-Cola advertising:

1886 Drink Coca-Cola.

1893 The ideal brain tonic.

1905 Coca-Cola revives and sustains.

1922 Thirst knows no season.

1929 The pause that refreshes.

1941 Everything your thirst could ask for.

1956 Coca-Cola, making good things taste better.

1960 Coke refreshes you best.

1970 It's the real thing.

1971 I'd like to buy the world a Coke.

1979 Have a Coke and a smile.

1982 Coke is it.

1985 New Coke.

1989 Can't beat the feeling.

1990 You can't beat the real thing.

1993 Always.

1998 Enjoy.

2001 Life tastes good.

2002 All the world loves a Coke.

Some of the slogans are trite, trivial, and silly. Coca-Cola was using "Enjoy" at the same time that Pepsi was using "The joy of cola." Together the two leading cola brands were spending $382 million a year to tell consumers to enjoy cola.

Only twice, in 1970 and again in 1990, did Coca-Cola go back to its roots and run the kind of advertising it should have been running. The kind of advertising that reinforces its heritage.

In 1970, Coca-Cola ran a television spot that opened with a visual of the Grand Canyon. "There are over three thousand canyons in the world, but only one they call Grand. When you find the real thing . . . on the road, in a museum, or in the refrigerator . . . you know it."

In addition to the opening scene of the Grand Canyon, the visuals consisted of icons like the Statue of Liberty, the Empire State Building, Niagara Falls, and the Golden Gate Bridge. Also a Rolls-Royce, a Harley-Davidson, the Mona Lisa, a diamond engagement ring, a slice of apple pie, an ice cream cone, and naturally an ice-cold bottle of Coca-Cola, the real thing.

If Coca-Cola had been a football team, the fans in the stands would be yelling, "We're the real thing!" They wouldn't be shouting things like "Enjoy" or "Always" or "Life tastes good" or "All the world loves a Coke."

An old idea, especially if it's emotional, resonates in the mind. A new idea, especially if it's original, is usually met with skepticism.

The perception of Coca-Cola as the real thing is also why New Coke was such a disaster. It undermined the brand's credentials, exactly the same mistake Coors made with Coors Light and its Elkton brewery.

Going Off Course at Callaway

The product that made the brand famous was the Callaway Big Bertha driver. But golf clubs were not good enough for Callaway.

Callaway Golf spent $170 million to build a plant and infrastructure to manufacture a new golf ball, which it called the Callaway Rule 35 golf ball. Then they spent another small fortune hiring Arnold Palmer to promote the ball.

Sales of the Callaway Rule 35 golf ball the first year were a minuscule $3 million.

Going against the golf ball market leader (Titleist) with a line-extension name (Callaway) is bad enough. But trying to accomplish this almost impossible task with an advertising program is the height of foolishness.

(Good brand names, like St. Charles Consulting, often contain the seeds of a good story. Why did you call your new golf club the Big Bertha, Mr. Callaway? Because the club reminded me of the cannon the Germans developed in World War I to throw shells on Paris from 70 miles away.)

So what does the Rule 35 mean? Not much. It is so named to call attention to the 34 rules that set limits on the size, specifications, and performance of golf balls.

As companies grow up, they tend to forget what made them famous. The Callaway Big Bertha was a major success because of a new category, a new name, and a powerful PR campaign. Advertising played only a minor role. When a company gets big and successful

(Callaway is by far the leading golf club maker), it thinks it can short-circuit the process by going directly to a big advertising launch.

Callaway needs advertising today not to launch golf balls, but to protect its leadership position in golf clubs.

In our consulting assignments, we have worked with many companies like Callaway Golf. They know that line extension doesn't generally work, but if they can find one exception to the general rule, that's a good enough reason for them.

- Because General Electric successfully line-extended its name, they can do it, too.
- Because Nike was able to take a meaningless theme ("Just do it") and make it memorable, they can do it, too.
- Because Wal-Mart was able to sell everything, they can do it, too.
- Because Microsoft was able to take a No. 2 brand (its browser) and make it the leader in its category, they can do it, too.

It's like saying that just because someone won the $100 million lottery, you can do it, too. True, but the odds are against you. Furthermore, your company's position is likely to be different from these examples. In most situations, your company is not Nike. Not Microsoft. Not Wal-Mart. And not General Electric.

Take our word for it. You can always find at least one exception to every rule. You have a choice. You can either live by the rules and accept the possibility that you might miss an opportunity because you didn't break one of the rules. Or you can live a life of anarchy.

Going Off Course at Xerox

One of the biggest mistakes in marketing is trying to use advertising to line-extend a brand.

- Nike athletic shoes, Nike golf clubs
- Tanqueray gin, Tanqueray vodka
- Heinz ketchup, Heinz salsa

Line extension is especially dangerous if advertising is the key way the line-extension product or service is communicated. Xerox, one of the most technologically advanced companies in the world, tried to market a line of Xerox mainframe computers. Then they tried to market a line of Xerox personal computers. Both products failed.

In both cases, Xerox relied on advertising to communicate its computer messages. But advertising has no credibility with buyers. "Xerox computers? That doesn't make sense. Xerox is a copier company."

Xerox has credentials in copiers. Xerox has no credentials in computers. And advertising is not going to provide the credentials for either mainframe or personal computers. These credentials have to come from PR efforts. It's as simple as that.

The "me, too" aspects of these products also hurt Xerox's ability to broaden its brand. Xerox wasn't first in computers. They didn't seem to have much of a competitive angle. As a result, the publicity generated was neutral at best. Success or failure rested entirely on the advertising.

If you are depending on advertising alone to make your brand successful, your brand is in deep trouble.

Going Off Course at Amazon.com

Amazon.com is a brand built on publicity. At one point, Amazon was getting mentioned in more articles than Bill Clinton. But those days are long gone.

Today Amazon needs advertising to maintain and enhance its brand. But as a book brand, not as a Jeff-of-all-trades brand. This is especially true because book sales at Amazon have been relatively flat lately.

Amazon should be pulling out all the stops with book fairs, bookmobiles, Amazon-sponsored seminars with famous authors, Amazon terminals in libraries, and of course, Amazon advertising to drive its book business. Amazon's goal should be to take its 7 percent share of the book business and make it 25 percent.

Instead of using advertising to boost its book business, Amazon is trying to use advertising to expand into other categories.

Results have been awful. If Amazon were a drugstore or a department store or a physical retailer of any kind, investors would be screaming for Jeff Bezos's head. (Sure, by the dint of superhuman effort, Amazon.com was able to turn a tiny profit in the fourth quarter of 2001. But will Amazon continue its winning way? We doubt it. One quarter does not a dollar make.)

But not at Amazon.com, the poster boy for the new economy. Don't worry about it, seems to be Jeff Bezos's attitude, we have enough money to tide us over until we break even and become profitable.

It doesn't matter how much money you have, if you lose money long enough, you're going to go bankrupt. Make no mistake about it, Amazon is headed for history's scrap heap unless the company changes its strategy. Amazon keeps throwing advertising dollars at the problem without backing off and reevaluating its strategy.

Advertising is not good for building a brand, and advertising is not good for changing a brand once it's built.

"This is not your father's Oldsmobile" didn't lower the average buyer age of an oldsmobile buyer.

"This is not just a book buyer's Web site" is an advertising idea with as much chance of success as the Oldsmobile program.

Amazon's only hope would be a PR program, and even that would be difficult. Why doesn't Amazon drop the advertising and use PR to establish a broader position?

The answer is always the same. "We can't wait for a publicity campaign to work. We have to move rapidly before someone else beats us to the punch."

It's a real dilemma. On the one hand, the long-term winner is usually the brand that gets into the mind first. On the other hand, publicity programs take a while to work.

So companies try to short-circuit the process by using advertising to force their way into the mind. One can understand their reasoning. But one cannot understand their willingness to pursue a strategy that doesn't work. You can't ask advertising to do publicity's job.

According to analysts, Amazon makes money on its core business: books, music, and videos. What it loses money on are the rest of the products and services it is trying to peddle. And what a list it is: auctions, baby supplies, camera and photo supplies, cars, cell phones and service, computers, computer software, electronics, health and beauty aids, kitchen and housewares, magazine subscriptions, outdoor-living equipment and supplies, tools and hardware, toys and games, and travel.

Amazon's core business accounts for 58 percent of its sales. What if Amazon narrowed its focus to books, music, and videos? If you were an accountant, you would make a decision like that in a flash. If you were *Time* magazine's 1999 Person of the Year, as Jeff Bezos was, you might find it a hard pill to swallow.

The good thing about narrowing the focus and going back to basics is that you don't have to give up any of your other products. All you have to do is to launch as many brands as you need to have each brand stand for something in the mind.

Keep in mind that brands are built by publicity. A new brand has much more publicity potential than a line extension of an old brand. New brands like Lexus, Dockers, DeWalt, Palm, and BlackBerry generated tons of publicity.

Polaroid, Xerox, and Kodak

Amazon can always retreat to its core business, but other companies don't have the security that a profitable core business provides. Take three recent examples: Polaroid, Xerox, and Kodak.

All three of these brands are associated with product categories that are past their prime. Polaroid with instant photography, Xerox with plain-paper copiers, and Kodak with film photography. All three companies are trying to do the same thing as Amazon is trying to: broaden the brand to include other lines of products.

History demonstrates that this solution doesn't work. The more memorable the brand name, the more difficult it is to change what the brand name stands for in the mind.

Western Union stood for telegrams, but the market dried up, so Western Union tried to get into the long-distance telephone business. Although Western Union was a better-known name than Sprint or MCI, the company never made it in the phone operations. After losing $600 million, Western Union shut down its phone business and retreated to its money-transfer business.

To borrow a line from F. Scott Fitzgerald, there are no second acts in branding. Once a brand is strongly established in the mind, it is difficult to change the perception of the brand. What should a company that owns one of these legacy brands do? Launch a second brand.

It may be too late for Polaroid, Xerox, and Kodak, who have driven down the single-brand highway for so long they can't see the advantages of a second brand. But Amazon still has a chance. Amazon is a young company, not set in its ways like the old folks at Polaroid, Xerox, and Kodak. We'll see.

Smirnoff vs. Absolut

Yet management of many other big companies sit behind their barricades buttressed by their big advertising budgets secure in the knowledge that no upstart can threaten their kingdoms. They forget about PR. Advertising is no defense against a PR program launched by a new brand in a new category.

Heublein, owners of Smirnoff vodka, the second-largest-selling liquor brand in America, turned down the opportunity to distribute Absolut vodka on five separate occasions.

As a Heublein executive explained, "If those Swedes come here and try to introduce one of those superpremium vodkas and threaten our Smirnoff, then I'll introduce the world's most expensive vodka, a Smirnoff de Czar, and kick the shit out of them."

As sales of Absolut exploded, Heublein did indeed launch a superpremium vodka, called Smirnoff Black. But Smirnoff Black failed to knock the feces out of Absolut, which continued its upward climb. (Smirnoff is now owned by Diageo, the world's largest spirits company.)

Going Off Course with Line Extensions

A line extension will almost never overtake a new brand that has achieved some publicity momentum.

- Did the Hewlett-Packard Jornada overtake the Palm handheld? No.
- Did Heinz salsa overtake Pace salsa? No.
- Did Bayer acetaminophen overtake Tylenol? No.

- Did the IBM personal computer overtake Dell? No.
- Did the Motorola cell phone overtake Nokia? No.

Why do companies launch line extensions instead of launching new brands? It usually boils down to money. We can't afford to launch a new brand.

When you dig deeper, you find that advertising is at the heart of the matter. It's the cost of advertising the new brand that keeps companies on the line-extension treadmill.

New Brands vs. Old Brands

That's ironic. New brands should be launched with publicity, not advertising. It's the old brands that need the advertising, which is the oxygen in their life-support systems. New brands need the credibility that only publicity can provide.

New brands need publicity. Old brands need advertising. But age is not what makes a brand old. If the brand is nowhere in the mind, then it is a "new" brand as far as the prospect is concerned, even though it might have been on the market for decades.

If you are trying to change an old brand's position, then it might just as well be a "new" brand as far as marketing is concerned. Change needs a PR approach, not an advertising approach.

Advertising and PR can live together happily ever after, but only if each discipline accepts its legitimate role in the marketing family.

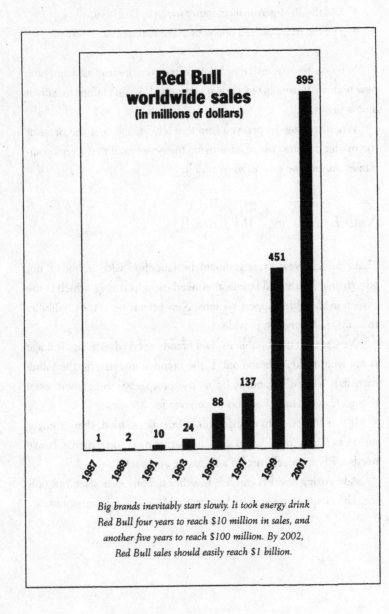

Red Bull
worldwide sales
(in millions of dollars)

1	2	10	24	88	137	451	895
1987	1989	1991	1993	1995	1997	1999	2001

Big brands inevitably start slowly. It took energy drink
Red Bull four years to reach $10 million in sales, and
another five years to reach $100 million. By 2002,
Red Bull sales should easily reach $1 billion.

23

Firing On
All Cylinders

Brand building is slow, patient, methodical work. It takes several decades, goes the old saying, to become an overnight success.

Sure, there are some exceptions, which we call shooting stars (Microsoft is one). But these exceptions usually take place in industries that are exploding in growth, carrying the leading brands along with them. In the vast majority of cases a brand takes many years (or many decades) to successfully establish itself.

Take the energy drink Red Bull. The brand was launched in Austria using primarily PR and merchandising techniques and only switched to advertising after it had gained considerable momentum.

It took Red Bull four years to reach $10 million in sales. Today, Red Bull does almost $895 million in annual sales and has become a big advertiser. When you try to jump-start the brand-building process with advertising, you run into trouble.

Building a Retail Brand

Take Wal-Mart, a company that started its retail operations in 1945. (It didn't adopt the Wal-Mart name until 1962.) Fifteen years after its founding, Wal-Mart had nine stores doing $1.4 million in sales. A decade later, Wal-Mart did $31 million. A decade later, $1.2 billion. A decade later, $26 billion. A decade later, $193 billion.

By next year Wal-Mart is likely to be, in terms of sales, the largest corporation in the world.

It takes time, you might be thinking, to build an organization. It takes time to find the right people to hire. And it takes time to obtain the necessary financing. To a certain extent all of these things are true. But they are not the real barrier to building a brand.

The real barrier is the human mind. It normally takes decades to build a brand because it takes decades to penetrate the gray matter in between your ears.

That's why many of today's most powerful brands have been around for quite a while. General Electric, the world's first electric brand, dates back to 1892. Mercedes-Benz, the world's first automobile brand, to 1885. Wedgwood pottery to 1759. Moët & Chandon champagne to 1743. Rémy Martin cognac to 1724.

The Wal-Mart brand started slowly using traditional small-town publicity techniques. Parades with marching bands, cheerleaders, drill teams, floats. Wal-Mart was also big on contests, everything from poetry to singing to babies. On theme days, everyone in the store dresses in costume.

Today, of course, Wal-Mart spends half a billion dollars a year on advertising, but not to build the brand. (The brand has already been built by public relations.) The money goes to defend the brand against the likes of Kmart and Target.

A brand spreads by human contact, much like a common cold. It takes publicity or PR activity to start the process moving (and to keep it moving), but once the process starts, you need to allow enough time for "word of mouth" to complete its task.

Changing a Mind

There's another reason brand building can be a lengthy process. To build a new brand, you often have to change the prospect's mind about an old brand.

When was the last time you changed your mind? Last week? Last year? Or can't you remember? Most people can't remember ever changing their mind because they believe their mind holds nothing but the "truth." To change your mind means to admit to yourself that one of your "truths" turned out to be a falsehood. That's hard for most people to do.

When evidence to the contrary piles up over a number of months, or even years, a person can slowly accept a new truth and forget that he or she ever held a contrary point of view.

This is the most important point. It's the "forgetting" of the old truth that allows a person to accept a new truth. You need to allow enough time for this forgetting to take place.

Editors are people, too. They see revolutionary PR concepts exactly the same way as your prospects do. It's new, it's different, and it's instantly under suspicion. You need to allow enough time to pass to let these objections fade away.

You need to allow enough time to pass to let editors be influenced by what they see, read, or hear in other media.

Building a Sports Drink Brand

Gatorade is a $2 billion brand with 79 percent of the sports-drink market. Gatorade was the key brand at Quaker Oats when the company was bought by PepsiCo for $14 billion.

If you haven't studied soft-drink history, you might assume that Quaker Oats launched Gatorade with a multimillion-dollar advertising program. Nothing could be further from the truth.

In the sixties a University of Florida team of researchers headed by Dr. Robert Cade developed a drink to replace fluids and body salts. They tested the drink on the university's football team, the Florida Gators. After a winning 1965 season, the Gators became known as a second-half team because of their endurance. When they defeated their Orange Bowl opponents, the losing coach said, "We didn't have Gatorade. That made the difference," a quote that wound up in *Sports Illustrated* magazine.

That was the magic moment, the publicity coup that kick-started the Gatorade campaign. Eventually Gatorade went on to become the official drink of the National Football League, the National Basketball Association, the Professional Golf Association, NASCAR, and many other sports associations and events.

Over the years Gatorade has maintained this continuity between PR and advertising, including the traditional ceremony of pouring a bucket of Gatorade over the head of the winning football coach.

Like its sister brands, Pepsi-Cola and Mountain Dew, Gatorade today is a heavily advertised, TV-oriented soft-drink brand. For a number of years Michael Jordan was the Gatorade spokesperson. "Be like Mike" was the theme.

What's the cause and what's the effect? Did Michael Jordan make Gatorade a successful brand? Or did the success of the Gatorade brand generate enough money for the company to hire Mr. Jordan as the brand's spokesperson?

Advertising, especially television advertising, is the mark of success in the corporate world. Advertising is like a corporate jet. It's the success of the company that allows it to buy a Gulfstream jet and not vice versa. So, too, with advertising.

Does that make advertising (or a corporate jet, for that matter) a poor investment? Not at all. Advertising is a poor investment for a brand just getting started. Advertising is a great investment for a "king of the hill" or leader brand.

You might be shocked to learn how much it costs Gatorade to maintain its connection to the NFL. Yet it is exactly marketing investments like this one that make it almost impossible for Powerade or All-Sport to ever overtake the sports-drink king of the NFL hill.

Not a Tool for Mind Changing

Advertising has another characteristic that makes it unsuitable for changing a mind, which is exactly what you need to do when you are launching a new brand. In terms of impact per dollar, a small dose of advertising is not as efficient as a large dose.

The easiest thing to hide in America today is a million dollars' worth of television advertising. Nobody will ever notice a dose that small. If you don't spend enough money to get above the noise level, your entire advertising investment is going to be wasted.

That's why advertising agencies push for the "big-bang" launch. Their only hope to make an impact is to spend enough money to break through the apathy that consumers have toward advertising. (It's an advertising rule of thumb that a viewer has to be exposed to a TV commercial at least three times before he or she will understand and remember the message.)

The big-bang approach might be a good idea for an advertising campaign, but it's a poor strategy for getting into a human mind. You don't hammer an idea into a mind, you let it seep in.

Successful brands get into the mind slowly. A blurb in a magazine. A mention in a newspaper. A comment from a friend. A display in a retail store. After a slow publicity buildup, people become convinced that they have known about the brand forever. (When did you first learn about Gatorade? Who can remember?)

Building a Whiskey Brand

The first registered distillery in America was the Jack Daniel Distillery. Located in Lynchburg, Tennessee, the company has received barrels of publicity since its founding in 1868. Every year about 250,000 people visit the distillery to gaze at the charcoal mellowing vats and the iron-free water that flows from an underground spring at a constant temperature of 56°F.

Wisely, Jack Daniel's advertising reflects and reinforces the perceptions created by Jack Daniel's publicity. A typical billboard says: "134 years. Seven generations. One recipe."

When you visit the Lynchburg distillery, you are struck by the thought "Looks just like the advertising!" How creative is that? In spite of a longtime trend to vodka, gin, and tequila, Jack Daniel's has become the seventh-largest-selling liquor brand in the world.

Jack Daniel's is a good example of a brand that has made a smooth transition from publicity to advertising. In particular, the advertising reflected and reinforced ideas first introduced by its PR campaigns. The advertising may have been uncreative, but it was both effective and efficient.

The first registered brewery in America was Yuengling. Yuengling? With a name like that, it was certain that Gentleman Jack would be in the whiskey hall of fame and Mr. Yuengling would be lost in the hallways of hops history.

Building a Small-Car Brand

In 1999, *Advertising Age* selected the top one hundred advertising campaigns of all time. No. 1 on the list was the 1960s program for Volkswagen. Legend would have you believe that Doyle Dane Bernbach took an unknown car brand and made it into an enormous success. But Volkswagen was hardly an unknown brand before DDB took the Beetle for the advertising ride of its life.

Volkswagen arrived in the United States in 1949, the same year Doyle Dane Bernbach was founded. Over the next decade, Volkswagen generated many favorable stories in the press, including a glowing review in *Consumer Reports*. By 1959, Volkswagen was the largest-selling imported car in America. That year Volkswagen sold 120,442 cars in the United States, which represented 20 percent of the import car market.

The next year "Think small," DDB's first ad for Volkswagen, ran, and the rest is marketing history.

As powerful as the advertising was, Doyle Dane Bernbach didn't start from scratch. Nor should they have. Advertising needs the credibility created by publicity. Volkswagen advertising did what advertising does best. Take a successful brand and make it even more successful.

What would have happened if advertisements like "Think small" and "Lemon" had run in 1949 instead of 1959? Probably nothing. The "small, ugly, reliable" themes were first created by publicity and then used in the advertising to "fan the flames."

Advertising is like a joke that exploits existing perceptions in the mind. If you make a joke about Drew Carey's weight ("Carey is carrying a heavy load"), the joke isn't funny if the audience is thinking, "Who's Drew Carey?"

Volkswagen's "Lemon" advertisement captured the reader's attention because he or she believes the opposite. Why are they calling the most reliable car on the road a lemon? "This Volkswagen missed the boat," reads the copy. "The chrome strip on the glove compartment is blemished and must be replaced. Chances are you wouldn't have noticed it; Inspector Kurt Kroner did."

"Oh, I get it," thinks the reader. "One reason that Volkswagens are reliable is the thorough inspection that each car receives."

Furthermore, the credibility of the advertising was reinforced by the general knowledge that you needed to get on a waiting list for a Beetle, you had to pay full price for the car, and you had to sell your old car yourself because most VW dealers wouldn't take trade-ins.

It was those perceptions in the mind (reliability, waiting list, full price, no trade-ins) that made the Volkswagen advertising so powerful.

Suppose, however, this were an advertisement for a Yugo. Same layout, same picture, same headline, same copy, same creativity. Would the reader think, "Wow! I didn't know Yugos were so reliable?"

Of course not. The reader would most likely think, "Who are they kidding? The Yugo is a disaster."

Advertising doesn't build brands. Advertising doesn't even put new ideas into people's minds. Advertising takes old ideas that already exist in their minds and reinforces them or ties them together or plays with them. Cheerleading has nothing in common with communications.

Were the Volkswagen ads creative? By current standards, probably not. In two decades of advertising, Volkswagen didn't use a single animal, the acid test for creativity.

Look at award-winning advertisements in particular. These ads are presumably the best the industry has to offer. Would any of these advertisements be effective if the basic idea in the ad wasn't already in the mind of the reader or viewer?

Building a Safe-Car Brand

In 1996, a Volvo ad won the Grand Prix at the International Advertising Festival in Cannes, the most prestigious advertising awards competition in the world. It was a print ad with no copy, just a visual of a safety pin shaped like a Volvo.

Did readers say, "What in the world is a safety pin doing in an automobile ad?" No, they knew exactly why the safety pin was there. "Isn't that cute. A safety pin bent into the shape of a safe car."

If you bent a safety pin in the shape of a Chevrolet (assuming you could figure out what the shape of a Chevrolet was), would that make an effective illustration for a Chevrolet ad?

Volvo introduced the first safety belt for automobiles in 1959, and five decades later Volvo advertising is still taking advantage of the brand's publicity achievement.

The Slow Buildup at Volkswagen

All brands, even monster brands, start small. Volkswagen was no exception. Six years after its introduction, Volkswagen sold less than 30,000 cars in the United States.

Not until thirteen years later, in 1968, did Volkswagen top out as a brand. That year Volkswagen sold 564,000 cars in the United States, or 56 percent of the imported car market.

In other words, it took nineteen years for Volkswagen to peak as a brand. The first ten years were primarily publicity years, the following nine years were primarily advertising years. Publicity first, advertising second is almost always the best branding strategy.

The combination of a slow buildup and an initial need for publicity rather than advertising has made some big agencies shy away from handling new brands. Advertising might be the way great brands get to be great brands, but try walking into a big 4A agency with a new product and a small budget. Then say to the new business director, "Help me build a great brand."

The big agencies we used to work for actively discouraged their account people from soliciting new brands. What they wanted were existing brands, preferably with existing king-size advertising budgets. It's a fact that most monster brands got started with small agencies and then switched to big agencies when the brand got successful enough.

The Slow Buildup at Absolut

Absolut is a monster brand, one of the hundred most valuable brands in the world. But Absolut's first advertising agency was Martin Landey, Arlow, a small New York firm. After two years of hard work the Swedish vodka was selling fewer than 25,000 cases a year.

Then Martin Landey, Arlow was bought by an agency called Geer, Gross, who promptly resigned the Absolut account because they already had a liquor account, Brown-Forman. (Big mistake.)

After partner Arnie Arlow left to become creative director at TBWA, another small agency, he helped TBWA acquired the Absolut account and rode it to the top. Eventually TBWA sold out to Omnicom, the world's third-largest advertising conglomerate with revenues of more than $6 billion a year.

Did Omnicom build the Absolut brand? Or did Omnicom buy bragging rights to the Absolut brand?

Big companies don't generally create big brands either because they don't have the patience to wait out the long gestation period that brand building usually requires. It's been our experience that most big brands got started by small companies that eventually sold out to larger companies. And most big brands were initially handled by small agencies who either lost the account to a bigger agency or were eventually bought by one.

We're not negative on advertising. It has a powerful role, which we define as cheerleading, or reinforcing the brand's perception in the prospect's mind.

Patience and Fortitude

In essence, building a powerful worldwide brand that dominates a major category requires only two things: patience and fortitude.

You need patience to let the PR people build the brand using the power of publicity, or third-party endorsements. Sometimes you get lucky because your brand is in a hot new category. The explosive success of the personal computer industry made the Microsoft brand. Not vice versa.

But most times, things move more slowly. Look at liquor. It took decades for gin to replace whiskey as the libation of choice. It took decades for vodka to replace gin. And it will take decades for tequila to replace vodka.

You need patience to avoid trying to force the issue with advertising. TiVo and Replay, for example, have wasted millions trying to buy their way into the integrated TV club. This is money that could have been much better spent on PR and product development.

The XM and Sirius satellite-radio people are also making the same mistake.

You need fortitude to keep your brand narrowly targeted. The biggest mistake any company can make is to try to broaden the appeal of a brand when they should be trying to "deepen" it. You need to be strong somewhere rather than weak everywhere.

Flexibility and Boldness

No one can predict the course of a PR campaign. The target market for your new brand might change. The major attribute of your new brand might change. The distribution might change. You need flexibility to deal with these and many other issues.

Volvo thought that durability would be the major benefit of its brand. Yet the publicity built Volvo into the "safe car" brand. Wisely, Volvo shifted its marketing program to emphasize safety to deemphasize durability..

When you do get your lucky break (and everyone gets one lucky break to go along with your fifteen minutes of fame), be prepared.

Be prepared to seize the moment. Plant your brand flag on the idea you have established in the mind and then have the boldness to launch an advertising program to secure that position for the foreseeable future.

Anita Roddick was a personal publicity machine who built The Body Shop into a global brand. But she didn't have the stomach for spending millions of advertising dollars protecting the "natural" cosmetics position she once owned in the mind.

So today The Body Shop is floundering, under attack by competitors like Origins, Bath & Body Works, and Aveda and on the verge of being sold. Recently, Anita and her husband, Gordon Roddick, resigned as cochairmen and the company called off sales discussions because of a lack of interest among potential buyers.

It's hard. Yesterday advertising is bad for the brand. Today advertising is good for the brand. How can one person cope with a situation like this?

Take heart. If you are a marketing manager, that's why they pay you all that money.

PART FOUR

The Differences Between Advertising and PR

1

Advertising Is *the* Wind.

PR Is *the* Sun.

In one of Aesop's fables, the wind and the sun had a dispute over who was the stronger of the two.

Seeing a traveler walking down the road, they decided to settle the issue by trying to make the traveler take off his coat. The wind went first, but the harder the wind blew, the more closely the traveler wrapped his coat around him.

Then the sun came out and began to shine. Soon the traveler felt the sun's warmth and took off his coat. The sun had won.

You can't force your way into the prospect's mind. Advertising is perceived as an imposition, an unwelcome intruder who needs to be resisted. The harder the sell, the harder the wind blows, the harder the prospect resists the sales message.

Advertising people talk about impact. Spreads, inserts, foldouts, and full color in print ads. Frenetic action, crazy angles, and jump cuts in television commercials. Turning up the volume in radio spots. But these are exactly the attributes that say to a prospect, don't pay any attention to me, I'm an advertisement.

The harder an advertisement tries to force its way into the mind, the less likely it will accomplish its objective. Once in a while a prospect drops his or her guard and the wind will win. But not often.

PR is the sun. You can't force the media to run your message. It's entirely in their hands. All you can do is smile and make sure your publicity material is as helpful as possible.

Nor does the prospect perceive any force in an editorial message. It's the opposite. Prospects think that media are trying to be helpful by alerting them to a wonderful new product or service.

2

Advertising Is Spatial.

PR Is Linear.

Advertising campaigns are like military campaigns in the sense that they are usually built around a launch date. (D day, June 6, 1944, the day that Allied forces landed in France during World War II.)

Both advertising and military campaigns usually start on a given launch date, but in different "spaces." In a military campaign, it might be air, water, beaches, trenches, etc. In an advertising campaign, it might be broadcast, print, direct mail, billboards, an incentive program for the sales force, etc.

This is what we mean by a "spatial" program, one of the key elements in current advertising thinking.

But when the smoke clears away, when the excitement of the initial launch is over, usually nothing much has changed. The prospect's attitude is the same as it was before the launch. It's difficult to force your way onto a heavily defended beach. It's almost impossible to force your way into a mind.

PR programs are inevitably linear. One thing leads to another. In a linear program, the elements unfold over time. The advantage, of course, is that they can be designed to work together to reinforce each other.

The trouble with most advertising programs is that they don't go anywhere. There's no unfolding of elements, no buildup, no climax, no drama, no "What's going to happen next?" excitement.

Which is why the beginning of a new year usually marks the start of a new spatial advertising program. With a new objective, a new strategy, a new advertising theme.

This annual advertising changeover is just the opposite of good branding strategy.

3

Advertising Uses
the Big Bang.

PR Uses *the*
Slow Buildup.

It's become an article of faith among advertising people that an advertising program needs to be launched with a "big bang." Especially for a new brand.

When you are trying to build a new brand, you need to accomplish a lot of things at once. Capture attention, register the name of the new brand in the mind, and attach one or more positive attributes to the new brand.

It's a big job that advertising is unsuited for. PR is a much better choice.

In fact, if you are launching a new brand with a PR program, you have no choice. You have to use a slow buildup, as there is no way you can coordinate media coverage. You start small, often with a mention of the brand in some obscure publication. Then you roll out the program to more important media. If you're lucky, you wind up on the *Today* show, *Moneyline*, or maybe even *World News Tonight*.

When you study the history of the world's most successful brands, you are struck by how slowly they started. In its first year, Coca-Cola sold $50 worth of syrup. For many decades Coca-Cola remained primarily a drugstore "fountain" brand.

Today we think of the Coke bottle as the essence of the brand, but it took forty-two years before bottle sales of Coca-Cola surpassed fountain sales.

The most successful single personal-computer model (in terms of units) was the Apple II, which eventually sold in the millions. Yet in its first two years on the market, only 43,000 Apple IIs were sold.

4

Advertising Is Visual.
PR Is Verbal.

The biggest advertising guru on Madison Avenue has been dead for 2,500 years, but his mantra is embedded in the mind of every creative person there.

Advertising people worship at the shrine of Confucius and repeat his mantra: "A picture is worth a thousand words."

As a result, advertising today is almost totally visual. The words are there just to reinforce the visual. Like the frogs who croak, "Budweiser."

Words have little credibility in an advertisement. The company that shouts "We're the best" convinces no one. "That's what they all say" is the typical consumer's reaction.

Advertising has backed itself into a visual corner. You can argue with the words, but you can't argue with a picture. No one is going to think, "That's not a frog."

Motivation is another matter. The mind thinks with words, not pictures. Prospects decide which brands to buy based on verbal comparisons. It's the best, it's the cheapest, it's the biggest, it's the lightest, it's the safest, it's the hippest, etc.

Joe Sixpack doesn't ask the bartender for "the beer that Louie the lizard drinks." No, Joe Sixpack asks for a Bud and thinks, "The king of beers, the best-selling beer in America, the beer that all my buddies are drinking."

The essence of public relations is to verbalize the brand in a way that encourages the media to run stories about the product or service. If pictures are used at all, they are supportive of the words. They lend credentials to the message.

The press release for Volvo's new $85 million safety center in Gothenburg, Sweden, for example, included a photo of a crash test. The picture supports the safety position of the brand.

How can advertising become more verbally oriented and hence more effective? Only by focusing on words and ideas previously established in the mind by publicity techniques.

5

Advertising Reaches Everybody.

PR Reaches Somebody.

It's an axiom of the advertising industry that you need to reach everybody. Reach and frequency are the twin measures of advertising success. (How many prospects do we reach and how frequently are we reaching them?)

Many advertising programs are mathematical successes and marketing failures. The client might be reaching everybody he or she wants to reach with enough frequency to create boredom and still not move the merchandise. You can't motivate a purchase if the message lacks credibility.

With PR you give up the luxury of reaching everybody in favor of reaching somebody who counts. Somebody who will carry your message to friends, relatives, neighbors. (Most brands are first purchased because of personal recommendations, not because of advertising or even publicity mentions.)

The emphasis in PR is not on reach and certainly not on frequency. The emphasis in PR is on the credentials of the medium and the quality of the plug. You need both. (A favorable mention in the

Wall Street Journal is worth a lot more than a lavish plug in some minor publication.)

Recently the Mini Cooper ended its forty-one-year run when car No. 5,387,862 came off the production line, a remarkable record for a single automobile model.

Yet the Mini Cooper sold poorly until Peter Sellers bought one and customized it with wicker trim. Suddenly the Mini Cooper became the "in" car. Steve McQueen, Twiggy, Princess Grace, Princess Diana, and many other celebrities drove Minis.

You don't have to sell everybody, you just have to sell Sellers. This is the strategy used in successful PR campaigns.

6

Advertising Is Self-Directed.

PR Is Other-Directed.

A company launching an advertising campaign has decided what it wants to be, what it wants to sell, and whom it wants to sell it to.

A company launching a PR campaign literally puts its future in the hands of others. It's the media who will be telling you what you are, what you should be selling, and what sales approach you should be using. You ignore these directives at your peril.

The media put Volvo into the "safety" seat. For many years Volvo was focused on durability. Typical Volvo ad headline: "Drive It Like You Hate It." The copy claimed that Volvos lasted an average of thirteen years on Sweden's rugged roads. This durability claim was backed by the fact that nine out of ten Volvos sold in the United States were still running.

But Volvo's invention of the three-point lap-and-shoulder safety belt generated so much publicity that Volvo slowly backed into "safety" as its marketing theme. A good move. Thanks to safety, Volvo has been selling well over 100,000 cars a year in the U.S. market alone.

Letting the media dictate your marketing strategy might seem to be the height of foolishness. Yet what choice does a company have? You can't fight the press. They'll win every time.

In dealing with the media, you need to be flexible. "If at first you don't succeed, try, try again" is not a good motto for a PR program. Persistence pays off with animosity as far as the media are concerned. (Al was once called a "commie nut" by the advertising columnist of the *New York Times* when he had the nerve to argue a point. That was bad enough, but he was also banished from the column for two years. You have a better chance to win an argument with your spouse than you have with the media.)

A better motto for a PR program is "If at first you don't succeed, try something else."

7

Advertising Dies.

PR Lives.

Nothing is as useless as yesterday's advertisement. It might wind up on the wall of an ad agency or in a book of award-winning ads. But as far as the average consumer is concerned, an ad is a butterfly. It lives for brief moments and then it dies.

Not so with publicity. A good story will live forever. The fundamental PR strategy is to use a story in one publication and then move it up the ladder to another publication. Or from one medium (print) to another medium (radio or TV).

You can also run a story down the ladder. The *Wall Street Journal* is a good example. A story in the *Journal* will often also wind up in one form or another in dozens of lesser publications.

The computer and the Internet have accelerated this process. Before writing a story on a new product or a company, a reporter will often check to see what other publications have written about the subject. An endorsement in one publication might be reflected in many others in the years ahead. (Nobody, we hasten to add, ever checks old advertisements.)

In PR today, it's important to get the first story right. Human nature being what it is, all the stories that follow are likely to be heavily influenced by that first placement.

The media operates like a human mind. Once a set of words gets established in the media, it will be exceedingly difficult to change them. "Billionaire Ron Perlman" is how the media refers to the entrepreneur who controls Revlon. With Revlon sagging and his other investments tanking, it's been years since Mr. Perlman has been a billionaire.

Yet as far as the media is concerned, it's still "Billionaire Ron."

8

Advertising Is Expensive.

PR Is Inexpensive.

Most companies spend considerably more money on advertising than on PR. Sometimes by several orders of magnitude.

That doesn't necessarily make PR look like a good investment. Some people who wouldn't spend $100 on a Timex will willingly spend $5,000 on a Rolex. Value and price are often firmly linked in the mind. The higher the price, the greater the value.

We recently had lunch with the brand manager of a hot company who wanted to hire us in the worst possible way . . . except that he couldn't afford our fee. He pleaded with us to cut our price. Naturally we said no.

One week later we read in the *Atlanta Journal-Constitution* that the same company had hired an advertising agency to launch a $50 million advertising campaign. The advertising apparently was worth $50 million to the client, but the consulting services weren't worth the $50,000 we were going to charge them.

As luck would have it, our consulting advice would have been to cancel the advertising program and establish a PR position first.

In general, clients are overspending on advertising and underspending on PR. In particular, clients need to spend more PR time and money on strategy development and verbalization.

A PR program should also operate over a longer time. You don't launch a PR program. You let it unfold in a series of steps over an extended period of time.

9

Advertising Favors Line Extensions.

PR Favors New Brands.

The biggest issue in marketing today is neither advertising nor PR. It's "line extension." Putting the company or brand name on a new product in a different category.

Amazon books. Amazon electronics.

Kodak film cameras. Kodak digital cameras.

AT&T long-distance phone service. AT&T cable service.

Look at a new product from the corporation's point of view. Kodak sees the eventual decline of film photography and decides to get into the digital field. Question: What brand name do we use?

The advertising guys are quick to respond, "We spent $116 million advertising the Kodak brand last year. It would cost at least another $100 million a year to introduce a new brand. Let's save that money and stick with the Kodak brand."

In our consulting work we have dealt with dozens of Kodaks. Invariably the mind-set is always the same. It costs too much to introduce a new brand. (Meaning, of course, the advertising to launch the new brand would cost too much.)

Advertising agencies usually go along with line-extension thinking because it means they get to keep the account. A new brand often means a new agency. Honda hired a new agency to introduce the Acura·brand. Ditto Toyota and Lexus; Nissan and Infiniti.

New brand or line extension? The cost of advertising should not be a reason to prefer a line extension. New brands should not be introduced with advertising anyway.

Beyond everything else (the product, the features, the benefits), a new brand needs credentials. This is a job only PR can do.

10

Advertising Likes
Old Names.

PR Likes
New Names.

While a new brand name is a liability in an advertising program, it's an asset in a PR program. A new brand name tells the media that the product or service is new and different. Exactly what the media want to write and talk about.

When Apple Computer introduced the Macintosh, it could have called its new product the Apple IV. But the Apple name would have buried the revolutionary nature of the new Macintosh product.

A new name greases the skids of a PR program. It implies that the product or service is so different that a completely new brand name is required. A line-extension name implies more of the same.

When Sony wanted to get into the video game business, it didn't call the brand the Sony VGP. No, Sony launched PlayStation, which generated mammoth amounts of media attention and soon became the leading brand of video game.

Contrary to conventional wisdom, the success of a second brand often depends on the ability of a company to divorce the second brand from the first. Carpenters and plumbers don't buy DeWalt tools because they are made by Black & Decker. Carpenters and plumbers buy DeWalt tools in spite of the fact that they are made by Black & Decker.

A new brand name breathes life into a PR program.

11

Advertising Is Funny.

PR Is Serious.

Advertising has a problem. It's a communications technique that lacks credentials and is almost universally ignored by its intended audience. How do you capture the prospect's attention with an advertising message?

Tell a joke. Be funny. Be entertaining. So Electronic Data Systems tries to sell multimillion-dollar computing contracts by herding cats on the Super Bowl, followed by a commercial about the running of the squirrels in Pamplona.

Advertising has a serious problem. The joke-laden, wise-guy approach has been falling on deaf ears. While the advertising industry pats itself on the back and repeats the punch line from the latest hot commercial, consumers are ignoring the messages. When was the last time someone actually said to you, "I'm going to buy a product I saw advertised on prime-time TV last night?"

Oddly enough, consumers do buy products advertised on television, but they are usually advertised on infomercials, which are consistently serious in tone. In addition, direct mail advertising, which lives or dies on results, is seldom humorous.

Building a brand is serious work that requires a thoughtful

approach. How do we define the category so we can be the first brand in a new category? What brand name do we select that's reflective of the category, yet is still a proper name? How do we approach the media so they will do stories about a new brand that's just getting started? Who is the spokesperson for the brand? What point of attack would ignite that single spark to make the brand take off?

These and other questions are serious. And herding cats or running squirrels is not the answer to any of them.

Sure, PR can be lighthearted, self-depreciating, and fun, but never funny. Leave the jokes to the advertising folks, who need them to win their next award.

12

Advertising Is Uncreative.

PR Is Creative.

You might be thinking that we got these headlines reversed. After all, the advertising industry prides itself on its creativity.

But what is creativity? In its purest sense, creative means "original." But advertising should not be original. Its role and function is not to insert new ideas into the mind, but to work with existing ideas put in the mind with PR techniques. And especially to reinforce these ideas. (This is the essence of the positioning concept we introduced thirty years ago.)

Unoriginal doesn't mean unskillful, unpolished, or unprofessional. Nor does it mean unclever. What advertising needs to do is to rein in its creativity and get back to cheerleading.

Contrary to popular opinion, creativity is not always a positive attribute. Creative accounting, for example, is exactly what got companies like Enron in trouble.

Creativity doesn't belong in the advertsing department; creativity belongs in the PR department. PR needs to be original in the sense that it needs to position products or services as new and different. "All the news that's fit to print," claims the *New York Times*.

The *Times*, along with other media outlets, doesn't want to write about better products or services. They want to write about "what's new." This means, what's original, what's different, what's creative.

The task of PR is to take the latest product improvement and with a generous dose of creativity turn it into something really new and different.

13

Advertising Is Incredible.

PR Is Credible.

The high point of the Siegfried & Roy show at the Mirage in Las Vegas is when the master magicians turn a tiger into a showgirl. Incredible, thinks the audience, absolutely incredible.

Advertising creates the same impression. When the polar bear drinks the Coca-Cola, the viewer thinks what a cute, clever, incredible commercial.

Advertising, like the Siegfried & Roy show, is incredible in the dictionary definition of the word: "not credible, unbelievable." No matter how much you camouflage an advertisement with creativity, at its core it remains a message with little credibility.

PR has a credibility problem, too. Do people believe everything they read, hear, or see in the media? Of course not. But there is an important distinction. They only reject information that conflicts with ideas already established in their minds. For example, Democrats will reject information that supports a Republican viewpoint. And vice versa.

Consider the situation when a new brand is launched, especially a new brand in a new category. There are no conflicts in the prospect's mind because there are no competing brands. It's a new category.

That's why PR is such a powerful tool in the launching of a new brand. Ideas can move from the media into the mind of the prospect with little chance of rejection. (If you don't know anything about a new product or a new category, why would you reject the information offered to you about the subject? If you don't know anything about Afghanistan, you will believe everything you read about the country.)

If you don't know anything about a new product or category, then you will believe everything you read about the subject, especially if the information comes from a credible source and not an incredible one.

This is why brand building via PR is such a powerful tool.

14

Advertising Is Brand Maintenance.

PR Is Brand Building.

We end with the heart of the matter. Advertising has a brilliant future if it accepts its true role in the life cycle of a brand. After being built by PR techniques, a brand needs advertising to maintain its position.

People forget. You need to constantly remind them of where the brand fits into the overall scheme. The king of beers. No. 1 in tires. The real thing. So easy to use, no wonder it's No. 1. America's favorite ketchup. Italy's No. 1 pasta.

PR, on the other hand, needs to move up the branding ladder. It needs to seize responsibility for its true role and function in the marketing process. Building a brand.

Brands live and brands die. A brand won't last forever. Ultimately every company will face the same problem. How to build a new brand to replace an old one as the old brand reaches the end of its life cycle.

Palm, BlackBerry, Starbucks, Red Bull, PlayStation, Nokia, Zara, Viagra, Amazon, eBay. These and many other new brands were created, not by advertising, but by publicity.

This is not an age issue. Some brands have been around for decades, but have never gotten into the prospect's mind. As far as marketing is concerned, these are new brands that need a liberal dose of PR before they can turn to advertising for support.

PR first, advertising second. This is the key to success in today's marketing arena.

PART FIVE

Postscripts

P.S. *for* Management

In the normal course of events, a discipline like advertising evolves over time to maintain its functionality. Evolution should have kept advertising from ascending into the ethereal world of art.

But it didn't. What kept the advertising function from adapting to a changing world? Two factors.

No. 1: The dominant dog factor. The idea that advertising is the dominant dog in the marketing household. Many managers see advertising and marketing as synonymous. The media typically refer to the "advertising and marketing community." *Advertising Age* calls itself "Crain's International Newspaper of Marketing."

A public relations agency is just a public relations agency, but a marketing agency is invariably an advertising agency with an upgraded name.

When you have been the dominant dog in the marketing community for more than a hundred years, you are going to resist an attempt to put your specialty at the back of the pack.

The advertising community is not going to give up its primary role in brand building without a fight. You can count on it.

No. 2: The creativity factor. The idea that the best advertising is the most creative advertising.

After years of beating the drum for creativity, the nation's advertising community has convinced itself and its clients that advertising has to be creative or it won't work. (Copywriters and art directors don't work in the copy/art department, they work in the creative department.)

Creativity is not just a goal of art directors and copywriters hot to win awards; clients love it, too. (You can't fault the company's advertising if a couple of Gold Lions sit behind the desk of the company's advertising manager.)

If advertising is going to be reborn as an efficient marketing discipline, these two positions have to be overturned in the minds of management. Let's take a look at both.

Everyone knows that advertising has an ego problem; the most typical complaint about advertising people is that they are "arrogant." Advertising people just naturally assume that advertising "sets the tone" for a marketing program. Before a company launches a marketing program, it turns to its advertising people to develop the strategy and the positioning theme to be used in the campaign. Or as they say on Madison Avenue, to come up with "the big idea."

The big idea in this book is the reversal of roles. The idea that PR should come first and advertising second. The idea that PR is the dominant dog in the marketing ménage and should set the strategy. And that advertising should follow that strategy once it is set in stone in the prospect's mind by the media.

What? PR people should set the marketing strategy that advertising people should follow? It will never happen, you might be thinking.

You might be right, only time will tell. But there's also a reason you might be wrong. Brand building takes place inside the prospect's mind. And only the media have the credibility to plant a new idea in the mind. If you are going to build a brand from scratch, only the media can do the job.

No brand starts from a position of strength. All brands were built from scratch. The essence of brand building is to furnish the materials that allow the media to build the brand. This is the essence of the PR business today.

There comes a time, however, when a brand runs out of publicity potential. When launched, a brand was probably new, exciting, and different. (Think Red Bull, for example.)

Brands, like people, grow up. They become old, boring, and the same. They need advertising to keep the brand alive in the mind.

But what kind of advertising? Here's where factor No. 2, creativity, comes into play. Brands don't need "creative" advertising (the brand has already been created in the mind by PR), they need "reminder" advertising.

Reminder advertising doesn't have to be dull and boring. If it were, it wouldn't do an effective job.

Reminder advertising can, and probably should, be clever, interesting, provocative, entertaining, exciting, dramatic, well written, well acted, and well produced. In short, everything you could possibly want in an advertising message *except* creativity.

P.S. *for* Advertising

If PR is superior to advertising for brand building, then why has there been so little written about the subject? That's a fair question.

"PR replacing advertising as the primary brand-building tool" is a story we haven't seen in any major publication. For a number of reasons, the fall of advertising and the rise of PR has received scant attention in the media.

First, and most important, is the strength and reputation of the advertising establishment. Advertising, narrowly defined, accounts for 2.5 percent of America's gross domestic product. Furthermore, advertising has its tentacles into newspapers, magazines, radio, television, the Internet, outdoor and direct mail. Advertising is as American as baseball, hot dogs, apple pie, and Chevrolet.

Then there are the organizations that stiffen the spine of the advertising establishment. The American Advertising Federation with 210 clubs and 50,000 members. The American Association of Advertising Agencies, whose membership includes 494 agencies with 1,279 offices, representing the country's most successful advertising agencies. The Association of National Advertisers represents 300 companies with 8,000 brands that spend over $100 billion a year on advertising.

The largest organization in the PR field is the Public Relations Society of America with 100 chapters and 20,000 members. There is no Association of National Publicizers, apparently because PR and publicity is not considered important enough. Some of the largest PR firms belong to the Council of Public Relations Firms, but the organization itself doesn't have the clout of the Four A's.

Second, people tend to judge the value of a discipline by its numbers. And advertising is a much bigger portion of a typical company's budget than PR. Take Dell Computer, for example. Last year Dell spent $430 million on advertising and $2 million on PR. In other words, Dell spent 215 times as much on advertising as on PR. It's going to be hard for Michael Dell to believe that PR is more important than advertising.

Yet Dell is a good example of a brand built by PR, not advertising. Early on, Dell made sure that computer analysts for all the trade publications received Dell machines for testing. *PC Week*'s rave review of the Turbo, Dell's first IBM-compatible machine, appeared shortly after the product was introduced in 1985. Almost immediately, the company began selling more than a thousand Turbo machines per month. And the rest is history.

Third, advertising benefits from extensive editorial coverage. Daily advertising columns appear in the *New York Times*, the *Wall Street Journal*, and the *Chicago Tribune*. Weekly ad columns appear in *USA Today*. None of the big national newspapers has a regular PR column.

Fourth, advertising and advertising people dominate the national scene. When Secretary of State Colin Powell needed someone to be in charge of the "public relations war" in the Middle East, whom did he select? Charlotte Beers, an advertising person who was the former head of both the J. Walter Thompson and Ogilvy & Mather advertising agencies. Headline in *PR Week* magazine: "The Mother of Ads Leads the Mother of PR Campaigns."

What does it say to the business community when you hire an advertising person to fight a PR war? (Hint: PR is a secondary function to advertising.)

Fifth, advertising dominates the educational scene. A recent Council of Public Relations Firms survey of seventy-four business school deans found that more than half of MBA programs offered coursework in advertising, but only twelve offered coursework in PR—the smallest number recorded among all marketing disciplines including sales promotion and direct marketing.

Sixth, what really undermines the stature of PR is that most of the larger PR firms are owned by advertising conglomerates. Nine out of the ten largest U.S. PR firms are owned by just three ad conglomerates: Interpublic, Omnicom, and WPP.

The only independent PR firm in the top ten is Edelman Public Relations Worldwide, which is No. 5 on the list. Even so, Edelman is more than twice the size of the next largest independent PR firm, Ruder Finn.

Two-thirds of all PR expenditures are handled by PR firms controlled by ad agencies. This is a major reason why so few voices have called for advertising to give up its brand-building role. How many PR executives are going to risk irritating their advertising bosses by proclaiming the fall of advertising and the rise of PR?

According to Jack O'Dwyer, publisher and editor of *Jack O'Dwyer's Newsletter*, "PR will always be a second-class citizen as long as the big PR firms are under the thumb of ad agencies."

When you are owned by your enemy, you learn to keep a low profile. Richard W. Edelman, CEO of Edelman PR, is the lone high-profile independent PR voice in a sea of advertising-oriented PR executives.

Look at the numbers. Advertising last year was a $243.7 billion business versus PR's $4.2 billion, a ratio of fifty-eight to one. (Advertising is the dog; PR is the tail.) And two-thirds of that $4.2 billion was spent with PR firms that are part of advertising conglomerates.

This book is our attempt to "wag the dog."

P.S. *for* PR

Our business is consulting with top management. Most of the ideas and concepts in this book were developed as a result of consulting sessions we have conducted with the management of major U.S. and foreign companies.

Yet one factor about most of these meetings was disturbing.

When we looked around the boardrooms, we saw mostly advertising people at the meetings. If PR people were in the room, they were mostly silent when marketing strategy was discussed.

We wonder. Has the shift from advertising-oriented marketing to PR-oriented marketing been welcomed by the PR industry? Perhaps not. Too many PR professionals talk of being an ombudsman, or the voice of the consumer inside the corporation, rather than the voice of the corporation itself.

Too many PR professionals would rather counsel the CEO than work in the trenches with the marketing folks. Too many PR professionals complain about the PR industry having "sold out" to marketing.

Sold out? How can you sell out to the most important function of a corporation, marketing? All other corporate functions exist to serve the marketing function.

Marketing doesn't exist to support manufacturing, for example. It's actually the reverse. Manufacturing exists to support marketing. In brand building, you can always "outsource" things like manufacturing and distribution.

(Malaysian sweatshops can be said to "outsource" their marketing function to Nike and Reebok. But where does the real power lie? In Kuala Lumpur or in Beaverton, Oregon? In the manufacturing or in the marketing?)

If a company's marketing activities are not working, then the company is in trouble no matter how good the PR counseling it receives. Would you rather be a successful son of a bitch or an unsuccessful prince of a fellow? The top managers I know invariably prefer the former to the latter.

Take Microsoft. Some PR professionals look at the company as a public relations disaster. Some disaster. Microsoft is one of the most valuable companies in the world, worth $364 billion on the stock market. Regardless of what happens in the courtroom, Microsoft will remain an enormous success, or perhaps several enormous successes, in the marketplace. (A company, by the way, built by publicity, not by advertising.)

Corporate managers are just beginning to recognize the power of public relations in the building of brands. They need to do more. They need to shift their thinking from an advertising-oriented mode to a PR-oriented mode.

In particular, PR professionals have a unique opportunity to seize the marketing reins of their clients, to become the leading source of outside marketing counsel, to become the driving force in the building of brands. Now is not the time to be bashful. Now is not the time for the reluctant bride.

PR is making progress. With the 1998 introduction of *PR Week*, the first "professional-grade" public relations publication, the industry now has its own trade paper comparable in scope, layout, and writing to the sixty-nine-year-old *Advertising Age*, the bible of the ad industry. Says editor-in-chief Jonah Bloom, "*PR Week's* rapid expansion in the U.S. and its increasingly global presence, with five offices in four continents, is a testament to the growth of PR as both a strategic business tool and a vital component of any marketing campaign."

It's not going to be easy. The small size and fragmented nature of the PR business is a serious detriment to this endeavor. Furthermore, the PR industry is dangerously divided over the role and function of PR. This is nothing new. In 1975, some sixty-five public relations leaders sat down to write a consensus definition of PR:

"Public relations is a distinctive management function which helps establish and maintain mutual lines of communication, understanding, acceptance and cooperation between an organization and its publics; involves the management of problems or issues; helps management keep informed on and responsive to public opinion; defines and emphasizes the responsibility of management to serve the public interest; helps management keep abreast of and effectively utilize change, serving as an early warning system to help anticipate trends; and uses research and sound and ethical communications techniques as its principal tools."

Eighty-seven words and not a single mention of what we consider to be the most important role of PR: building a brand.

In 2001, the Public Relations Society of America chose "The Power of PR" as the theme for its annual meeting. Here, according to PRSA, is why PR is powerful:

"The Power of PR addresses public relations as a process facilitating the exchange of value in our world: person-to-person, organization-to-publics, and society-to-society. The positive force of public relations promotes understanding, works toward agreement, and searches for mutual gains. Public relations professionals have the power to advance social agendas; help clients achieve their goals; and mediate, manage, and mitigate conflict."

Again, no mention of brand building.

Read again the theme of the American Advertising Federation's ad campaign: "Advertising. The way great brands get to be great brands." And you know the AAF is serious because they have trademarked the "great brands" slogan.

Everything is a brand. Coca-Cola is a brand. The United States of America is a brand. Public Relations is a brand. And how do you build a brand? You try to own a word in the mind. Coca-Cola is the real thing. The USA is the largest free country in the world. (Hence the theme: Enduring Freedom.) But what is PR?

According to one prominent PR pro, "Public relations is the art of earning and leveraging the trust of an organization's key stakeholders."

Come on, guys, you're not trying out for the part of the in-house guru. You have a job to do, perhaps the most important job in any organization. Building the brand.

In the long run, you also need to build the PR brand. You need to do what the AAF is trying to do. You need to own a word in the mind. Unfortunately, it's the same word as the one the advertising folks are trying to own. Brand building.

What's next? First you need to reposition the advertising function before you can position the PR function. (Part Three, "A New Role for Advertising," discusses this issue.)

What about the many other PR functions inside a company: corporate reputation, crisis management, investor relations, etc.? If you can't build a great brand, then all these other functions, no matter how skillfully handled, won't help a company achieve success.

Anyone who works for a corporation has to be a jack-of-all-trades. You might need to do planning, budgeting, report writing, and a dozen other tasks. But none of these tasks should divert your attention from the core objective of your specialty.

In the case of PR, that's brand building.

Index